RELENTLESS
OPTIMISM

Books by Darrin Donnelly

THINK LIKE A WARRIOR

The Five Inner Beliefs That Make You Unstoppable

OLD SCHOOL GRIT

Times May Change, But the Rules for Success Never Do

RELENTLESS OPTIMISM

How a Commitment to Positive Thinking Changes Everything

LIFE TO THE FULLEST

A Story About Finding Your Purpose and Following Your Heart

VICTORY FAVORS THE FEARLESS

How to Defeat the 7 Fears That Hold You Back

THE TURNAROUND

How to Build Life-Changing Confidence

RELENTLESS
OPTIMISM

How a Commitment to Positive Thinking Changes Everything

Darrin Donnelly

Cover design by Damonza.

ISBN-13: 978-0692921838
ISBN-10: 0692921834

Visit us at: SportsForTheSoul.com

Sports for the Soul

This book is part of the *Sports for the Soul* series. For updates on this book, a sneak peek at future books, and a free newsletter that delivers powerful advice and inspiration from top coaches, athletes, and sports psychologists, join us at: **SportsForTheSoul.com**.

The *Sports for the Soul* newsletter will help you:

- Find your purpose and follow your passion
- Use a positive mental attitude to achieve more
- Build your self-confidence
- Develop mental toughness
- Increase your energy and stay motivated
- Harness the power of positive self-talk
- Explore the spiritual side of success
- Be a positive leader for your family and your team
- Become the best version of yourself
- And much more…

Join us now at **SportsForTheSoul.com**.

To Laura, Patrick, Katie, and Tommy;
who are everything to me.

Introduction

Positive thinking leads to positive outcomes. Study after study proves this. Researchers have found that optimistic people live longer, live healthier, have more energy, have more successful careers, make better decisions, are more productive, are less stressed, have healthier relationships, and (not surprisingly) are much *happier* than pessimists.

However, a lot has been misunderstood about what it means to be a positive thinker and what it takes to maintain an optimistic outlook.

It requires more than repeating feel-good platitudes to make positive thinking work in your life. It takes discipline, commitment, and a proper understanding of what optimism really means in a world that is constantly throwing new challenges at us.

This is a book for anyone who has ever questioned whether positive thinking really "works."

It's also a book for those who have tried to develop a more positive attitude, but have found it easier said than done when it comes to eliminating the voices of fear, doubt, and cynicism.

This is a book for anyone who wants to put optimism to work in their life with practical, proven techniques.

In this inspirational fable, you'll meet Bobby Kane, a minor league baseball player who, at the age of 31, is coming to terms with the fact that his dream of making it to the majors is finally coming to a disappointing end. After more than a decade of battling through ill-timed injuries and unlucky setbacks, Bobby has had enough.

His dream, he believes, was not meant to be.

But, life has a way of throwing us life preservers right when we need them. And Bobby Kane's life preserver comes in the form of an unconventional manager named Wally Hogan.

On the surface, Wally may look like your typical former-big-leaguer-turned-minor-league-manager, but Bobby quickly realizes that he's never had a manager quite like Wally.

More mental coach than baseball manager, Wally

teaches Bobby that if you want to change your life, you have to first change your thinking.

As you'll see in this book, developing a positive mindset gives Bobby a renewed chance to make his dreams come true—not just in baseball, but in all areas of his life.

Baseball is a sport of failure. It's a profession where the most successful batters fail seventy percent of the time and the most successful teams have to endure sixty losses or more each season. To succeed in baseball, you must learn not how to avoid failure, but how to quickly bounce back from it—with optimism and perseverance.

That is what positive thinking is all about. It's about responding to life's obstacles with a positive, never-back-down attitude.

It's true in baseball. It's true in life.

Wally teaches Bobby what it means to be an optimist and what it takes to maintain a positive attitude through the ups and downs of life. He teaches him proven, real-world techniques for building and sustaining optimism. These methods have an immediate impact on Bobby's life and they will have an immediate impact on yours as well.

This book will show you just how powerful a positive attitude can be and it will teach you how to use positive thinking to make your biggest dreams come true.

Darrin Donnelly
SportsForTheSoul.com

"Self-confidence is the first step toward success. If you believe it, you can achieve it."

- TOMMY LASORDA, Two-time World Series Champion Manager and Member of the National Baseball Hall of Fame

"So many players enter the game with the same approximate skills. The difference is not aptitude but attitude."

- DAVE WINFIELD, 12-time MLB All-Star, World Series Champion, and Member of the National Baseball Hall of Fame

"Things have a way of working themselves out if we just remain positive."

- LOU HOLTZ, College Football National Champion Coach and Member of the College Football Hall of Fame

"Life's battles don't always go to the stronger or faster man. But sooner or later, the man who wins is the man who thinks he can."

- Vince Lombardi, Six-time NFL Champion Coach and Member of the Pro Football Hall of Fame

1

"Now batting for Omaha, right-fielder Bobby Kane," the public address announcer said over the loud speakers. As hometown announcers tend to do for the visiting team, he made this announcement in the most mundane voice he could muster.

"Kane is *zero*-for-three so far tonight," he added, making sure to emphasize the word, *zero*. His reminder of my dismal stats up to this point in the evening was not something you'd get away with in a major-league ballpark, but here in the minors things were different. The fans still in attendance seemed to appreciate his announcement as I heard a smattering of chuckles and heckles behind me.

We shouldn't even be allowed to play baseball in conditions like this, I thought to myself as I walked to the plate in the ninth inning. *What is with this place? It's May, for God's sake. It's not supposed to be freezing out here.*

As I stepped into the batter's box, I noticed the red-nosed third baseman blowing into his bare hand, trying to warm it up. It had snowed earlier this morning. *Snowed.* In May!

What am I doing here? I asked myself. *After all the years I've put into this game, here I am still stuck in Triple-A, playing for a team called the Omaha Storm Chasers in front of a few hundred remaining fans on a below-freezing night in Colorado Springs.*

You've really set the world on fire, haven't you, Bobby?

I took a few practice swings and watched my foggy breath as I exhaled. I was trying to take my mind off my stomach. Something wasn't right with it. It wasn't nerves, it couldn't be. I was way too experienced of a ballplayer to have nerves tying my stomach in knots. This was something different. It was in the pit of my stomach. A tight, twisting feeling that spread into my bones and sometimes made my forehead sweat.

I'd been dealing with it all spring and I was starting to lose patience with the team doctor who told me it was just anxiety and would fade away soon enough. It affected my entire body. My swing was way off because of it.

I made eye contact with the pitcher and noticed a confident twinkle in his eye.

Pitchers loved playing baseball in this kind of

weather. The cold, windy conditions were great for them, horrible for everyone else. Pitchers usually put up their best stats in early spring, especially when playing up north. In the minors, where ERAs tend to run higher due to smaller ballparks and smaller strike zones, pitchers need to make the most of the cold weather.

Batters hated this weather. Fouling off a fast ball in sub-freezing temperatures is not something you want to experience more than once in your career. I had already done it at least five times on this night. My forearms were still tingling from the jolt that pierced through my arms on each of those foul balls.

We were down, 2-3, with one out. We had a runner in scoring position at second, a 21-year-old fresh out of college with lots of speed. He had been called up to Triple-A after spring training. You could tell the organization was excited about this kid.

I had a chance to be the hero. A power shot safely into the outfield would move our runner home and tie the game. A home run would give us the lead and break my month-long slump.

The first pitch buzzed past me—a fastball right down the middle. Strike one. This was the first time

I'd faced this pitcher and I wanted to see what he had. A hell of an arm is what he had.

I stepped out of the batter's box and retightened my batting gloves—a ritual I'd been using between pitches for the last fifteen years, all the way back to high school.

Okay, I thought as I studied the pitcher. *You've shown me your fastball; you think you've enticed me. But I know what's coming next. Something low and outside or something fast and high. Either way, you want me chasing. Ain't gonna' happen, pal.*

I stepped back into the batter's box and noticed the runner at second digging in with a big lead off the bag.

What are you doing, rookie? You're already in scoring position. Now's not the time to show off your speed. Wait 'till I get the ball in play, then show us all how fast you are.

The second pitch was a low fastball. I swung late, cracking the ball foul and once again feeling that cold, piercing pain jarring up my arms and rattling through my body.

As I grimaced, I could've sworn I saw the pitcher smirk. I gave him an icy stare as I stepped out of the batter's box once again.

What happened next steamed me even more than

that pitcher smirking at me. As if being down in the count oh-and-two wasn't enough to mess with my head, the signal came in from the dugout to send our runner to third.

Why steal third now? He's already in scoring position. It's because they don't believe in me. They don't think I can get the ball in play. They expect me to strike out swinging. Thanks for the vote of confidence.

That pain in my stomach quickly returned and for a second I thought about calling timeout. It was now tight *and* queasy. I took a deep breath to calm the feeling. It worked. Kind of.

The next pitch came in low and outside. I laid off it as our runner sprinted from second to third. The catcher put the ball on a rope to third base and they tagged him out.

I looked over to the dugout and shook my head. *Nice going, fellas.*

Two outs now. One ball, two strikes. Nobody on.

My own team doesn't believe in me. And why should they with the way I've been playing?

I had spent the month of April batting a miserable .104 — that means I was getting a hit just one out of every ten times at-bat. I also hadn't hit a single home run in the first month of the season. I was supposed to be the team's power hitter, which means they could live with a lower batting average as long as I was hitting more home runs.

Was my power gone for good? Had my time passed? And why is my stomach churning again? I've been playing professional baseball for thirteen years; the days of having anxiety attacks at the plate should be long gone!

Self-doubt and worry consumed me as I repositioned myself back in the batter's box.

I need a big one here, I thought as I took an easy practice swing. *They're losing patience with me. If I don't get one over the fence soon, they just might send me packing. My career could be over at any moment.*

I should have been focused on the pitcher and the game scenario I was facing. I should've been watching the pitcher's release, trying to decipher exactly what was coming at me. But all I could think about was my slump, my uncertain future, my wife, Janey, and our two kids back in Massachusetts still living with Janey's parents. And my stomach. I was finally playing without any of the injuries that had nagged me for years and now this stomach issue came out of nowhere. *Why now? If ever I needed an injury-free stretch, now was the time!*

As negative thoughts bombarded my head, the pitcher fired another fastball right down the middle. I watched it go by.

Four pitches, three strikes, and the game was over.

Two hours later, I was sitting in a bus headed for Albuquerque. I couldn't sleep. Too much noise — both on the bus and in my head. My stomach was fine now. It only seemed to give me trouble right before an at-bat or sometimes when I woke up in the middle of the night.

A few of the guys on the bus were sleeping, but most were either playing cards or laughing at each other's exaggerated stories. While nobody *wanted* to be in Triple-A baseball, it was still just one step away from the majors and most of these guys were in their early 20s. They lived with the hope that they could get the call up any day now. And it was still early enough in the season that they were enjoying the bus rides, the team camaraderie, and the fact that, majors or not, they *were* getting paid to play baseball for a living.

Not me.

After failing to make the twenty-five-man roster for the Kansas City Royals during spring training, I was finally coming to terms with the fact that my career was winding down. I wasn't going to feed myself false hope any longer. I had missed my chance. My boyhood dream was not going to happen. Now, I needed to figure out what I was going to do next with my life.

What else would I be qualified for? I had no college degree, no special skills outside of baseball. I suppose I could work for my little brother's landscaping business like I did most off-seasons, but last year he could only afford to pay me minimum wage. I had put *everything* into making it in the big leagues of professional baseball.

When I was 20, I had no doubt my dream would come true. I was fueled by unbridled optimism and all my closest friends and family members were constantly feeding my hopes and dreams. They were all behind me. It wasn't a matter of *if* I'd ever make it big in the majors; it was a matter of *when*.

Over the years, after several close-but-no-cigar seasons in the minors, those hopes and dreams started sharing time with doubts and fears. *If it hasn't happened by now, will it ever?* Friends and family members, while still encouraging, had started asking me questions like, "What do you plan on doing after your baseball career?"

"After my career?" I would respond. "My career hasn't even started yet."

Polite, but uncomfortable, laughs would follow.

The average age of a player who gets called up from the minors to a major league team is right between 24 and 25. I had turned 31 this past offseason. I knew my days were numbered in the eyes of baseball's scouts and general managers. I was officially one of the "older guys" in minor league baseball.

When I was 21, my team manager had told me, "You're pressing too hard. You've got to have patience and let the game come to you. Almost nobody makes it to the majors when they're 20. Now, if you hit 30 and you're still in the minors, you're in trouble. *That's* when you need to worry. If you haven't made it by 30, you never will. But you've got plenty of time, kid. Don't worry, you'll get there."

I never forgot that brief conversation.

The young optimist I was back then wouldn't recognize me now. My doubts had overtaken my hopes. My worst fears had become reality.

How could I have been so naïve? I wondered to myself as the bus rolled down the interstate. *How could I have believed in such an unrealistic dream? I've let so many people down, so many people who were counting on me. What do I do with my life now?*

Little did I know that night—as I sulked in self-pity on a five-and-a-half-hour bus ride—that my world and my mindset would soon be changing in a big way.

2

The three-game road trip in Albuquerque didn't do much to help my confidence. Though our team won two of the three games, it was no thanks to me. I continued to struggle at the plate with just one hit over the three-game stretch. My batting average dropped below .100 for the season.

One of the things that had helped me stay employed in the minors for so long (despite occasional slumps at the plate) was my versatility on defense. I could play just about anywhere they asked me to. Through the years I had played mostly in the outfield, but also first base, second base, third base, and a little shortstop. I had even pitched an inning or two here and there—a practice that is not all that uncommon in the minors when teams have to scramble to fill out their bullpen due to last-minute call-ups and trades.

But now, even my defensive play was struggling. I recorded two errors during the three games in Albuquerque. Both errors were followed by bat-breaking tantrums when I got back to the dugout.

The guys were starting to keep their distance from me. I'm sure some were simply turned off by the anger and negativity radiating off of me. Others—though they wouldn't admit it out loud—were afraid my "unluckiness" might rub off on them. Baseball players tend to be superstitious and nobody wants to get too close to a guy who's slumping. Misery loves company and the cruel baseball gods had a way of making slumps highly contagious. The younger players didn't want to take any chances. I couldn't blame them.

When we got back to Omaha, my manager called me into his office. Fearing that I was about to be benched for a better-looking prospect, my stomach churned as I walked in and took a seat.

"I'm gonna' ask you this one more time and I want you to shoot me straight," he said. "Is the wrist bothering you again, Bobby?"

I had broken my wrist eight years ago and it had nagged me throughout my career.

"No, the wrist is fine," I said, which was the truth. "I know I'm struggling, but I'm working on it. Trust me, I'll get things turned around."

"That's why I called you in here," he said. "We think we can help you with that."

"I'm all ears," I said with a sigh of relief. Maybe I wasn't being benched after all.

"We think it'd be best if you go down to Arkansas for a while. We think it'd be a good place for you to work out whatever it is you're going through."

He was referring to Springdale, Arkansas, the home of the Northwest Arkansas Naturals, which was the Kansas City Royals' Double-A team.

I couldn't speak. So much for my momentary relief. I wasn't being benched with the Storm Chasers, I was being *demoted* down to Arkansas. I felt like I'd been punched in the gut. I couldn't catch my breath.

"It's not a big deal, Bobby. Lots of guys hit slumps at this point in their careers. Sometimes a change of scenery is the best way out of it."

I wasn't buying it.

"You're sending me *down*?" I asked. "Down to Double-A?"

"It's either that or you start riding the bench here, and I know you don't want that. The organization wants to get more at-bats for some of these younger guys they're paying big money for.

"If you're going to be in Double-A, Northwest is the place you want to be. Trust me. It's a fairly new team. They've put a lot of money into it. They have one of the best ballparks in baseball. Hell, it's nicer than ours. They have a new manager too, a guy named Wally Hogan. He's one of a kind. I think you'll like him."

His attempts to put a positive spin on the situation only made me madder.

"Bobby, nobody works harder than you do every single day," my manager continued. "I mean that. Your work ethic is second to none. And the truth is, the organization thinks that work ethic will be a great example for some of the younger guys down there. They need to see someone like you showing them how to work."

There it was. I hadn't been fired from baseball, but I might as well have been. Like the fictional character, Crash Davis, in the classic movie, *Bull Durham*, the organization no longer saw me as a player with potential. They now saw me as a glorified coach, someone who could be a "good example" to the *real* prospects.

"In August, you sat right in that chair and told me I was on the verge of being called *up*," I said. "You said it could happen any day. That call never came. And now, now you're sitting there telling me I'm being sent *down*?"

"Don't make this personal, Bobby."

My manager turned cold. In an instant, he went from offering up a glass-half-full perspective to being offended that I was trying to blame him for the demotion.

"You know I don't make these calls," he said. "They come from the top."

"You've got a hand in it."

"Like I said, don't make this personal."

I couldn't believe it. Just six months earlier I was fighting neck-and-neck for a roster spot on the American League champion Kansas City Royals. Now, I couldn't hold onto my spot with the Omaha Storm Chasers.

"Bobby," my manager called as I headed for the door. "If I was you, I'd be thankful you still have a job playing baseball."

I didn't respond.

As I walked back to my locker, I could see my teammates shifting their eyes away from me. They knew I'd just been given the news that every player dreads. They didn't know what to say. Words of encouragement would be disingenuous. It's one thing to tell a 21-year-old rookie not to worry, that he'll be called back up in no time. But a 31-year-old was another story.

Everyone in the clubhouse knew this would probably be the last time they would ever see Bobby Kane, that older guy who never lived up to his potential.

3

Heading into this season, I was questioning whether my baseball career was coming to an end. Being sent down to Double-A gave me my answer.

I had been sent from Triple-A down to Double-A for a few brief stretches during my career. This was usually after an injury or for some unique situation, like making room for a major-leaguer who needed some Triple-A playing time for a rehab of his own.

But this time, it felt like a *permanent* demotion. Teams don't send 31-year-olds down to Double-A and ask them to "mentor" younger guys if they're planning to call them back up next week, next month, or even next year.

For as long as I could, I put off the phone call I knew I had to make. About five hours into the six-hour drive from Omaha, Nebraska, to Springdale, Arkansas, I called Janey. To earn more money for our family, she had recently started working more shifts as a nurse. I caught her during one of those shifts. She wasn't exactly thrilled to hear from her husband.

"What is it, everything okay?" Janey asked urgently.

"Not exactly. I'm on my way to Arkansas. I'm going to be playing down there for a while."

Janey was silent.

"I know you and the kids had talked about maybe making a trip to Omaha to watch me play," I said. "Just wanted to make sure you hadn't booked flights or anything."

"You know we can't afford a trip to Omaha," Janey said. "I thought we went over this before you left for spring training."

"We did, I just thought...I don't know what I thought. I just wanted to tell you. It also means my pay is going to be a little lighter for as long as I'm down here."

"What pay?" Janey said sarcastically.

"Fair point," I said.

"Bobby, I'm sorry to hear this. I know you're disappointed. I'm disappointed too, but I've got to get going. John has an appointment this afternoon so I need to leave work early today."

"A doctor's appointment? Is he alright?" John was our three-year-old son.

"He's fine," Janey said. "It's just an annual checkup. You know, parent stuff. Well, maybe you don't know."

"Ouch," I said. "That's a low blow, don't you think?"

"You're right, sorry," she said quickly, though there was no mistaking that the apology lacked sincerity. "It's just that it never ends around here and I could use an extra hand. I have to go. Drive safe. Bye."

As she hung up, I thought I could hear a quiver in her voice.

Things had not been good between us for the past six months. There's a reason everyone discourages guys in the minors from getting married. The failed pursuit of my dream had finally taken its toll on our marriage. Janey had every right to be frustrated with me. *I* was frustrated with me.

Janey and I had grown up together in a small Massachusetts town where kids spent the winters shoveling snow and the summers playing baseball until the sun went down. Janey and I were high school sweethearts and the two of us planned on attending Boston College together. Though I'd grown up dreaming of playing for the Boston Red Sox, it looked like football was going to be paying the bills for me and I was offered a full scholarship to play linebacker for the Eagles. Those plans changed the summer before classes began.

After my bat got red hot and our high school team won the state championship, I started hearing from more and more major league scouts. They said they loved my hitting power and they wanted to know how serious I was about going to college. Though I'd committed to play football for Boston College in February, my first love had always been baseball. These scouts kept reminding me of this fact and telling me it wasn't too late to pursue a baseball career instead.

Still, I told them all that getting a degree was important to me and my family. These guys did this for a living and I suppose they could tell when a prospect said one thing and was thinking another.

In early June 2002, I got the call. I'd been drafted in the Major League Baseball draft. The fact that I was drafted was not a huge surprise. What did come as a surprise was how early I was drafted and the team that drafted me.

I was picked in the sixth round by the Boston Red Sox, the team I — and everyone else I knew — had grown up living and dying for.

The Red Sox offered me a $70,000 signing bonus to put off college and start playing minor league ball immediately. I thought about it for half-a-day and chose baseball over college. No need to negotiate. This was the Red Sox. *My* team. Where do I sign?

Though my parents were supportive, I knew they disagreed with my decision.

"Why not play football in the fall, baseball in the spring, get your degree, and *then* give pro baseball a shot?" my dad had asked me. "It's only four years and it'll go by like that."

"If it was any team but the Red Sox, it'd be different," I said at the time. Though, being the short-sighted 18-year-old that I was, the $70,000 bonus was impossible to turn down. It might as well have been $700,000 to me.

Janey supported my plans to chase my big-league dream. I think we both enjoyed the attention that came with being the hometown kid who was off to join the Red Sox.

Janey went to college while I worked my way up

through Boston's minor league system. I quickly became a hot young prospect in the organization. Coming in with a linebacker build, scouts were glad to see that I was more than just a big bat. I was athletic enough to play just about anywhere defensively.

Time and time again, I was told that my positive attitude was a huge asset. Especially in the minors — a place everyone is trying to get *out* of — coaches told me the can-do optimism I wore on my sleeve stood out.

It wasn't hard for me to be positive. I was living my dream and I was certain that it was only a matter of time before I'd be hitting home runs over the Green Monster in Fenway Park.

I progressed each summer — moving from short-season A to low-A to high-A to Double-A to Triple-A — just like you'd draw it up. Everything was going as planned.

In 2007, I got the call every ballplayer dreams of. I was 23 years old. It was May, the same month that Janey had graduated college. The Red Sox called me up in what was supposed to be the beginning of a long and prosperous career in the majors.

Life couldn't get much better for me and Janey, who was now my fiancé. We believed all those who told us that life in the minors was no place for a married man, so we decided we wouldn't set a wedding date until I was officially called up to the majors. After I got the call, we immediately set a date for the offseason.

My career was progressing right on schedule. We both believed the stars had aligned perfectly to ensure that our dreams would come true. We had no doubt about all the great things the future held for us.

But the ecstasy was short-lived.

I spent ten whole days in the majors. In those ten days, I racked up three errors, I had just two hits in sixteen at-bats, and I broke my wrist in an outfield collision—a play that accounted for one of those three errors.

I tried to mentally shake off my disastrous stretch in the majors.

"No big deal," I told Janey. "I'll spend the summer rehabbing, finish the season in the minors, and then be back with the Red Sox by the beginning of next season. You'll see."

That October, I watched the Red Sox—guys who were my teammates for ten days in May—win the World Series.

In December, Janey and I got married.

All our big plans were still on track, or so I thought.

I came into spring training with plans to show the team that my rehab was a success and I was better than ever. I was focused on earning a spot on the twenty-five-man roster heading out of spring. I *had* to make it.

But my performance in spring training fell way short of expectations—my expectations and the expectations of the Red Sox. The ball wasn't flying off my bat like it used to. My timing was off. I struck out often and when I did make contact, I hit a lot of pop-ups and weak grounders.

And *that sound*, that vicious crack that would echo throughout the ballpark after I hit the ball just right. *That sound* that scouts and coaches had long told me was a rare gift I'd been blessed with. *That sound* was gone.

Something was off. I knew it and the coaches knew it. They thought I had developed a hitch in my swing. My wrist may not have healed properly, they told me with concerned looks that said, *What are we going to do with this guy now?*

They decided pretty quickly what they were going

to do with me. Prior to the 2008 season-opener, I was traded to Cincinnati.

I was devastated. Boston was *my* team, the team I'd grown up cheering on. Playing for the Red Sox was a dream come true—like it was *meant* to be.

It turned out the dream was too good to be true.

I kept a brave face. "No problem," I told friends and family. "It's part of the baseball life. We don't get to choose who we play for."

But inside, I was angry and hurt. I felt the Red Sox were giving up on me. I told myself I was going to show them how wrong they were, but I also couldn't help but wonder if I'd blown my chance at the majors. *Was it only a matter of time before other teams realized what the Red Sox already knew—that I was damaged goods?*

For the first time, I questioned whether things were going to work out the way Janey and I had planned. *Was my career over before it ever really started?*

I ended up playing a very average season with Cincinnati's Triple-A team, the Louisville Bats. In the offseason, I was traded again—this time to Cleveland in another minor league deal. Though I had some hot streaks here and there during my two seasons with the Columbus Clippers, I still hadn't regained the *consistent* home run power I had once shown. I still hadn't regained the power I was originally drafted for. Would *that sound* ever come back?

I never sniffed a call-up. After the 2010 season, at the age of 26, I was released by Cleveland and nobody called to sign me.

The timing of such news is never good, but it hit me particularly hard because we had just found out Janey was pregnant. I was at a crossroads. I could either continue pursuing my dream of making it back to the majors or I could settle for a more conventional career path. Perhaps I could finally go to college or find a job that didn't require a college degree, maybe bite the bullet and work for my little brother's landscaping business.

After many long conversations, Janey and I decided I should not give up on baseball. That offseason, we moved out of the apartment we'd been living in and moved in with Janey's parents to save money.

I tried to stay positive and remind myself that I still had plenty of time to make it back to the big leagues, but my nagging wrist problems were starting to weigh me down and Janey could tell I was questioning my ability.

In another hard decision, Janey and I decided to use what was left of our savings to pay for another wrist surgery—this one by a surgeon who said he could give me back what I had lost. Insurance wouldn't cover the expenses since it wasn't a matter of function, but more a matter of reviving an unemployed ballplayer's career. I had the surgery and prayed it would get me back on track.

I worked out harder than ever in the offseason. I was determined not to quit on my dream.

4

Just before the 2011 season was to begin and I thought I might have to sign with an independent league team (an even lower-pay version of minor league baseball, which isn't affiliated with any major league teams), I was invited to an open tryout with the Texas Rangers and they saw enough to invite me to spring training.

The surgery had been a success and my wrist problems were behind me. My spring-training performance earned me a new minor league contract with the Rangers.

It was a fresh start and I intended to make the most of it.

Through half a season with the Round Rock Express (the Rangers' Triple-A team), I was on fire. I was batting .355 and had belted 14 home runs. My stats were getting attention and a call-up seemed certain.

That is, until I pulled my hamstring chasing down a fly ball in left field.

The injury wasn't devastating, but it was severe

enough to keep me out for a few weeks and delay any chances of a call-up. When I got back on the field, everything was off and I spent the rest of the summer trying—unsuccessfully—to get back into the groove I was in before the injury.

Once again, I had missed my opportunity to get back to the majors.

It was another cruel setback. It seemed so unfair. Right when everything was back on track, another pointless injury had ruined all my effort.

Our son, John, was born that offseason and although I was thrilled to be starting a family, the added pressure of providing for children made me even more anxious about my uncertain future.

My anxiety grew as I began to question more and more if a major-league contract was ever going to happen. I turned 28 and knew I was running out of time. I also started to feel guilty about my decisions. *Was I letting my family down by chasing this dream? Was I being irresponsible and selfish by going after this long-shot career?*

"How many bad breaks can a guy endure?" I asked Janey one night when I was feeling particularly down. I was questioning my ability and my faith. I felt like

God was handing me a raw deal in life.

Through it all, Janey tried to keep my spirits up. She told me how much she believed in me. She promised we would find a way. She continued to plan out our life as though there was no doubt I'd soon make it back to the majors.

Through the next season in Round Rock (2012), I struggled to stay healthy. If it wasn't a sore shoulder one week it was a sprained ankle the next. As soon as I'd get in a good rhythm at the plate, I'd suffer through an ugly slump. This is when the negative voices in my head started getting louder and louder.

You'll never get there, Bobby. You've missed your chance.

After those two seasons with the Rangers' organization, they gave up on me too. As soon as they released me, I was signed by the Kansas City Royals in another minor league deal prior to the 2013 season. I turned 29 years old and had officially crossed into "old guy" territory. The Royals must have figured there was nothing to lose. I was cheap enough to take a chance on.

It was at this point that I noticed myself turning much more cynical about the game I once loved and about life in general. The stress of more than a decade in the minors had taken its toll on my attitude. My hopefulness was fading fast.

The off-seasons back in Massachusetts consisted of working long mindless hours driving a snow plow and shoveling dirt for my little brother's company. Between work shifts, I'd go through exhausting workouts. I don't know if I was working out to prove I could still make it or simply trying to burn off all the rage that had built up inside of me.

Janey was now pregnant with our second son, Michael, and what should have been exciting news only added to the pressure. I felt like a failure, someone who couldn't adequately provide for his wife and kids.

More and more, I'd drop negative comments to Janey—comments about how cruel life could be, how unfair the baseball business was, and how much I regretted not going to college when I had the chance.

"I feel like I'm living a Bruce Springsteen song," I said to Janey one night. "Like trying to chase this stupid dream is worse than never having any dream at all."

I had reached a moment of despair and it was

finally starting to break Janey's spirits as well.

"This is so unlike you," she said. "When we got married, you were so full of hope and optimism. I miss that guy."

"Me too," I said as though I had no control over the situation. "Me too."

Life in the minors had worn me down. And it had worn down Janey as well.

We started having more arguments, even in front of our friends and her parents. We still loved each other, but the stress of my career — the financial stress of low minor league pay, the physical stress of long days for that low pay, the emotional stress of me being gone for eight months out of the year — it was all driving a wedge between us.

More and more, we talked about how much longer we could keep this up. I wasn't always sure whether we were talking about my career or our marriage.

Prior to the 2014 season (a season that would be my second with Kansas City's Triple-A affiliate in Omaha), my dad became uncharacteristically lethargic. We could all tell something wasn't right. A few weeks after noticing this change in demeanor, he died of a heart attack. It was a reminder of how fast life goes by and how abruptly it can change.

In one of the last conversations I had with my dad, he told me, "Don't give up on your dream, Bobby. I *know* you can make it happen. I don't know how I know, but I just do. Don't give up, son."

This was an out-of-the-blue pep talk. Looking back, I wonder if something inside was telling him his days were numbered. It's strange how things like that happen.

This was less than a month before spring training and his encouragement gave me a renewed burst of enthusiasm.

That season, I had a breakout summer with the Omaha Storm Chasers. At the age of 30, I found myself attacking the ball once again. I batted .298 with twenty-five home runs (a career high for me), and seventy RBIs.

Those numbers got me renewed attention within the organization. My manager told me I was now a "4-A" player. That is, someone the organization considers to be better than Triple-A, but teetering just below the majors. A 4-A player was someone everyone expected to be called up at any moment, especially in September.

On September 1 each season, a major league team has the option to expand its active roster from twenty-five players to as many as forty. Usually, the organization will call up about five or six guys at this crucial moment.

One week before that key roster-expansion date, I got hit with a 95-mile-per-hour pitch on the bottom of my left hand. It was enough to fracture my hand and keep me sitting for the final few days of August.

On August 31, just a few weeks after I had missed my second son's birth because I was playing baseball in Omaha, I sat in the clubhouse and watched five guys from our team head into the manager's office. Each one returned with watery eyes and big smiles. They had just heard the words they had waited their whole lives to hear—that they were being called up to play for a major league baseball team (and earn a major league baseball salary for at least a month).

In what was an annual ritual on a Triple-A team, everyone in the clubhouse congratulated each player who received the news he had worked so long and hard to hear. And with every hug, backslap, and handshake, we each silently prayed that we'd be the next one called up.

After five of my teammates received the news of a lifetime, I waited for my name to be called.

It didn't happen.

I went back to my tiny apartment that night, put my head in my hands, and cried like a baby.

I watched on TV as Kansas City won the American League Championship and went all the way to the World Series. Though the Royals lost in Game 7 to the San Francisco Giants, I couldn't help but wonder if I could've helped make a difference.

What if I had been called up and had played in the World Series? *What if* I had been the hero who hit a walk-off home run to win it all? *What if* I had earned a major league contract for the month of September *and* all the bonus money that comes with a run through the World Series—how much that would have helped me and Janey's financial situation and renewed our spirits?

The more I thought about missed opportunities, the darker these *what if* scenarios became.

What if I had just missed out on my last chance ever to make it back to the big leagues?

I spent the offseason replaying these *what if*s. I couldn't stop focusing on how close I'd been to making it to the majors. I replayed mistakes and near-misses from the season over and over again. Just a few more hits would've gotten my batting average to that coveted .300 mark. Maybe they thought I was injured worse than I was and if that nameless idiot pitcher hadn't thrown a fastball into my hand a week before call-ups, I would've had a spot on the roster. If just three more bombs had stayed fair, I would've hit twenty-eight home runs and led the Pacific Coast League in home runs for the season. *Surely they wouldn't have passed on a home run leader even if that guy was 30 years old, right?*

I would wake up in the middle of the night and question just about every life decision I'd made since signing with the Red Sox nearly thirteen years ago. I should have gone to college when I had the chance. If I had, maybe I'd be making piles of money working for some big firm in Boston right now. Or, maybe I would be living a quieter, more secure life teaching high school in my hometown and coaching football and baseball. Either way, Janey and I would be much better off.

I had put in so much time chasing this dream—time that I would never get back. Even if I hadn't gone to college, I should have left the game the moment Cleveland released me. I would've been young enough at that point that I probably could've still earned a football scholarship somewhere. Another bad decision.

The pain of these regrets caused me to grow distant in the offseason. I couldn't stop thinking that I had blown my *last chance ever* to get called up.

Instead of being thankful for the fact that the Royals had renewed my minor league contract for another season and enjoying the limited time I had with my wife and two kids, I often found myself staring into space, quietly agonizing over my blown opportunities and bad decisions. I could feel myself growing more and more bitter. The only time I felt alive was when I was punishing myself with grueling workouts in the gym.

I could tell my stoic demeanor was bringing down Janey. Just one year after gaining renewed hope from my dad, I was once again complaining about all the bad breaks and talking about how mad I was at myself for chasing "this stupid dream."

It had to be brutal for Janey to live with someone that had become this negative, someone always wallowing in self-pity. I wanted to stop thinking like this, but I couldn't. Everything that came out of my mouth was cynical and hopeless.

Just before I left for spring training to begin the 2015 season—yet another spring full of uncertainty and stress—Janey cried harder than I'd ever seen her cry. It was a cold February night when she told me, "I can't live like this any longer."

"What are you saying, you want to separate?" I asked.

She didn't answer.

"Oh, that's just great," I said. "Nice of you to spring this on me now, as if I don't have enough on my plate as it is!"

"I'm not saying that," Janey said. "I'm saying I miss the man I married. The guy who believed in himself and was sure that anything he put his mind to was possible.

"Where is that guy?!" she cried.

"That guy grew up and faced reality," I told her as I walked away.

All she wanted was some hope. Some sign that the Bobby Kane she had married would be coming back.

But I couldn't give it to her. I didn't believe that guy

ever *was* coming back.

That is, until a man named Wally Hogan changed my life.

5

Less than five minutes after walking into the Northwest Arkansas Naturals' clubhouse, I felt a forceful slap on my back followed by a booming voice.

"Wally Hogan, great to meet you!"

I turned around to shake my new manager's hand.

"Bobby Kane," I said.

"I know who you are." Wally smiled, one cheek full of sunflower seeds. "I gotta say, when I heard they were sending you here I couldn't believe our luck. Step into my office, will ya?"

I followed behind Wally as he talked over his shoulder at me.

"I saw you a few years ago playing in Round Rock, Texas. Man, you were killing the ball. You had a shot over right-center that still hasn't landed. I was a part-time scout then, but I told Kansas City, 'If we ever get the chance, we need to sign this guy. He's got something special. You can't teach that type of hitting power.'"

"Thanks," I said as we took seats across from each

other in Wally's office. I was a bit overwhelmed by his praise. It had been a long time since I'd heard someone talking about me that way, like I was anything more than a washed-up minor-leaguer who had missed his shot at the majors.

I could see right away that Wally was a man's man. He had an Arnold Palmer tan and a stout, barrel-chest build. He had massive forearms and a sturdy middle-aged gut, which he made no attempt to hide — almost like he was proud of it. He had the kind of thick firefighter mustache that was popular with ballplayers back in the 1980s. He walked upright and with a purpose. The man exuded self-confidence.

"We could sure use some of your power right now," Wally said. "I can't wait to see you swing the bat for us."

"I'm excited too," I lied. How could anyone be excited after being sent *down*?

"You're from New England, right? I can tell by your accent."

I nodded.

"They love their baseball up there. How about family? You're married, right? Got any kids?"

"Yes, we have two kids. They're all back in

Massachusetts."

"That's great," Wally said. "I think guys with a family are a little more motivated than others. And it's always nice having a family that supports you."

This was a surprising statement. Most people in baseball discouraged guys from starting families in the minors. We were often warned that the grind would be too tough on a family. My personal experience didn't dispute that warning.

Wally wasn't like the minor league managers I was used to. The minors are a place of transition and, just like the players, minor league managers usually don't *want* to be here. They're trying to work their way up like everyone else and they can't wait to get out of here. They're often just as stressed about their low pay and uncertain future as the players are.

The managers I'd had in the past were detached, by-the-book guys. They didn't want to get too personal. It was the nature of the business. A manager couldn't get too tight with a player, become best friends with him, learn all about his personal life, and then send the guy packing halfway through the season. Managers had to keep a certain distance. I understood that.

But this guy, Wally, he seemed genuinely interested in me. He also seemed *enthusiastic* about his job. Maybe it was because he was new here and everything seemed fresh. The minors hadn't beaten him down yet.

"So tell me," Wally said as he leaned back in his chair and playfully tossed a baseball to himself. "Why are you here?"

I wasn't sure how to respond. I wrinkled my eyebrows and said, "Why do you think? I'm here because the organization sent me here."

"Yeah, they asked you to come here and you obviously accepted the invitation. Why?"

"I don't remember being asked," I said. "They sent me down. What choice did I have?"

"You always have a choice. You're 31 years old. You're a husband and a father. You could do a lot of other things with your life besides play baseball 1,500 miles away from your family. The organization asked you to play here. You agreed. Why?"

"Is this a job interview?" I asked, making no attempt to hide my annoyance with his grilling.

"I ask all my guys these questions. I like to make sure we're all on the same page before we start working together. So…what's your answer? Why are you here?"

Realizing that Wally wasn't going to let me off the hook, I smiled and said, "I guess because I'm still being paid to play baseball. It may not be much, but I figure if someone is going to keep paying me to play I should milk that for as long as I can."

This was a textbook answer from a player who had been stuck in the minors for too long.

Wally gave me a courtesy chuckle. "Fair enough, but I bet there's a better reason than that. Why are you really here? What do you hope to gain from this experience?"

"To be honest, I've been questioning that myself," I blurted out. I was surprised by my own blunt answer. Something about Wally's persona pulled my guard down.

"I see," Wally said. "And I thought that might be the case."

I must have sounded like some burned-out ballplayer who had lost his passion for the game. I may have been exactly that, but I didn't want my boss to know it. I quickly tried to walk back my answer.

"Don't get me wrong, I'm thankful for this

opportunity," I said.

I knew how expendable most minor league players were and I realized my less-than-enthusiastic answer could give the organization a good reason to cut me once and for all — and despite all my negative feelings at the moment, I wasn't ready for that to happen. Not yet, anyway.

"I intend to make the most of this shot," I said, but I didn't sound convincing.

In that moment, I realized that what I was saying wasn't entirely a lie. As discouraged as I was about being sent down to Double-A, there was still just a glimmer of hope left in my tank — hope that somehow, someway I could turn things around and earn my way back to the majors. The dream had faded, but it wasn't dead. It may have been on life support, but it wasn't *dead*.

"That's good," Wally said. "And I want to help you make the most of your time here. But you have to tell me the God's honest truth. Don't B.S. me. Do you still love this game? Do you still believe you can make it?"

I searched for the truth. There was a time when I had no doubt that I'd make it in this sport I loved. But it had been too long since I'd felt that way. The baseball gods had beaten down my dream and I had slowly accepted that it was probably not meant to be — that I couldn't make it in baseball after all.

But did I really believe that? Did I *really* believe it was all over?

"To be honest, Wally, most days I don't know anymore." I instantly regretted my frankness, but decided it was time to put it all on the table. No taking it back. Time to see where I stood with my new manager.

"There's this voice in my head that has gotten louder and louder in recent years," I continued. "It keeps telling me that it isn't going to happen. That this game I once loved so much has a cruel way of turning your dreams into nightmares. That voice has gotten so loud that it's drowning out everything else. I don't know what happened to me. I never thought I'd think like this."

Wally leaned forward, squeezed his baseball with two hands, and smiled big.

"That's what I thought," he said. "And I'm glad to hear it."

"Glad?"

"Yes! It means the problem's not physical. It's mental. And we're going to fix it."

6

That night, I suited up for the Naturals in a home game against the Tulsa Drillers. Wally's desire to help me get back on track gave me just enough encouragement to hit a shot all the way to the wall in my first at-bat, which was good for a much-needed triple. Dusting myself off at third base, Wally gave me a fist pump in the air and I realized I was grinning on the baseball field for the first time this season.

For the night, I had four hits in five at-bats and helped our team win the game, 8-3. It's amazing what an encouraging word can do for a man's self-confidence.

"I thought you were supposed to be in a slump," Wally said to me in the dugout during the ninth inning.

I smiled and shrugged as Wally playfully shoved me with his forearm.

Excited about the performance, I called Janey that night. I wanted to tell her about this guy, Wally Hogan, and let her know that I'd finally had a good game. I actually had some *good* news to share with her.

She didn't answer and she didn't call back.

My slump-breaking performance was short-lived. The next night, I found myself overthinking at the plate and my stomach pains were back, throwing everything off. I chased curve balls, I watched perfect right-down-the-middle fastballs fly by me as I stood over them like a statue, and when I did make contact I was late and the contact was weak. It was everything I'd been doing since spring training started. I was back to my old self. Five at-bats, three strikeouts, no hits.

"We need to talk," Wally told me in the clubhouse after the game. "Meet me in the parking lot tomorrow morning before the team bus pulls out."

"Ah, man," I heard one of my teammates grumble from behind me. "Wally, if going oh-for-five gets him a seat on your bus, what do I gotta' do? Give up ten runs in two innings?"

"You start giving up ten runs and the only bus you'll be riding on is a Greyhound back home to California," Wally said to him as he walked back to his office.

"Yeah, yeah," my teammate said with a laugh.

Then I felt that same player swat my back with the

back of his hand. "You know I was just playing, right?"

I turned around and extended my hand to a teammate I hadn't formally met. "Bobby Kane," I said with a polite smile.

"Ricky Alvarez, pitcher," he said. Like everyone else in this clubhouse, this guy looked young enough to get carded at a bar. He may have been in his early 20s, but he could've passed for 18.

"What was that all about?" I asked. "Wally doesn't ride with the team?"

"No," Ricky said, as though I'd asked a strange question. "Do other managers?"

I laughed. "Every manager I've ever known. Is this your first season playing pro ball?"

"I played with an independent team and then did a stretch of rookie-league ball last year; this is my first Double-A team—the real deal."

"Well, Ricky, let me tell you. This Wally guy does a lot of things I've never seen other managers do."

The next morning I saw why guys like Ricky wanted to ride along with Wally. Next to the typical-looking minor league team bus idling in the parking lot was a luxury RV.

As I lined up with my teammates to load my gear in the bus, Wally pulled me out of line.

"Go ahead and throw that in my ride," he said. "I don't want my players getting in the habit of separating themselves from their gear on a road trip. Last thing we need is to show up in some town eight hours from home and realize one of our starters doesn't have his uniform."

I wanted to tell Wally that I'd been playing ball for thirteen years in this circuit and I knew fully well how to take care of my gear, but I thought better of it. I didn't want to do anything that could cost me a seat on his RV.

The inside of Wally's RV was just as high-end as it looked from the outside. A flat-screen TV, a fully-equipped kitchen, leather couches, a bathroom with a shower, and a bedroom in the back that looked bigger than the one Janey and I shared at her parent's house back home.

"Wow," I said, taking it all in. "They know how to take care of their managers down here."

Wally let out a laugh. "I wish. This is all on my dime. I told them if I was going to take this job, I had to do it *my* way. The days of me bunking up in crowded motel rooms are long over. Plus, this way my wife can join me when she wants to. My kids and grandkids also plan on coming along for a few road trips this summer."

"Wally, I get the sense you do everything *your* way."

"You got that right. Doing what everyone else is doing and thinking like everyone else is thinking rarely works out well in life. At least that's been my experience. But this bus does serve a more important purpose. It's my office on wheels. These road trips are where some of my best coaching is done."

Wally pointed a remote at the TV screen in the living area of the RV and clicked it on, displaying a paused image of me swinging at a pitch from last night's game.

"Before we head out, I want to show you something," he said. "I noticed a problem with your swing in the first inning last night. Do you see it?"

I checked my hand placement, my wrist rotation, my hips, all the normal checkpoints, and nothing stood out as different from the way I'd been swinging the bat for the past decade-plus of baseball.

I shook my head. "It's the same as it's always been

for me."

"I don't think so," Wally said. "You're late on pitches, which is causing you to make weak contact or miss altogether. And the reason for that is your head placement."

"What's wrong with my head placement?" I zeroed in on the image of my head and didn't notice anything odd. I had my eyes on the ball, just like I'd been taught to do since I was five years old. Easier said than done, sometimes, but the image on the screen showed my eyes locked in as they should be.

"You're swinging uphill," Wally said. "You're doing that because your head is moving back and upward. See it now?"

He clicked a button on the remote and the image advanced frame by frame. I stepped closer to the screen and did notice my head pulling back. It was a very slight movement, but Wally was right.

"I see it," I said. "But I think I've *always* swung like that."

"No, you haven't," Wally said matter-of-factly.

He clicked a button on the remote and the frozen image of me came to life as I whiffed on the pitch. Ugly. Then a new frozen image of me popped up on the TV. This was me during my stint in Round Rock, either 2011 or 2012.

"Notice the difference?" Wally asked.

Sure enough, my head was tucked downward — just a bit — with my eyes again locked in on the ball.

"I'll be damned," I said.

Wally clicked the mouse again and let the video play. This time, I crushed the ball deep over the left field wall.

"And here's one from last year," Wally said as an image of me wearing an Omaha Storm Chasers uniform appeared on the screen. Once again, my head was tucked downward slightly more than the first clip he showed me.

"It's small, but it makes a huge difference, as you can see," Wally said.

He clicked a button to let the video of me slamming another home run continue.

"That's it?" I said with some excitement in my voice. "*That's* why I've been so far behind this season?"

"That's it," Wally said. "That's the mechanical reason, at least. Start making sure you tuck your head lower at batting practice tonight. Make sure you do it in the game and you'll see instant results. I guarantee that."

The certainty in Wally's voice made me anxious to get into a batting cage and start working on this change as soon as possible.

"But it's such a small tweak," I said. "It can't be that simple. It can't be the only reason I've been struggling so much this year."

"Most solutions *are* simple," he said. "At least, on the surface."

"What do you mean?"

"I mean that a player's swing doesn't just change overnight. Something *causes* it to change. Often it's a physical cause, like an injury or muscles wearing down. But I've watched you close, in person and on film, and your problem isn't physical. I'm sure of that. I saw you in the weight room yesterday and I saw you warming up before last night's game. You're probably the strongest guy on the team. You've still got all the physical tools you need."

"I'm glad one of us thinks so," I said sarcastically. "But if it isn't physical —"

"Then it must be mental," Wally said. There has to be a reason you changed the mechanics of your swing, a subconscious reason. Your head placement is the solution right now. Like I said, you'll have instant results from fixing that issue. But it's a short-term fix. When the problem is a mental one, it'll find a way to screw up other parts of your swing. It's only a matter of time. The mental stress caused by negative thoughts always invokes a physical reaction somewhere. Pretty soon we'll be chasing one mechanical flaw after another in a never-ending scramble to fix your swing. That is, unless you fix the *mental* cause of these problems.

"Fix the mental, and the physical will follow."

I was starting to wonder if Wally was a baseball manager or a shrink.

"When I watch you play, your whole body is tensed up," Wally continued. "Much tighter than you used to be. That's something that happens to most guys in a slump; they start trying to kill it, they play tighter, they hold the bat so tight it's like they're trying to squeeze sap out of it. It only makes things worse.

"But with you, it's something more than just the urgency of a slump. Something inside of you — something in the pit of your stomach, in the back of your mind, or both — is tearing you up. I know you feel it. Am I right?"

I nodded and looked down at the floor, as men in this line of work tend to do when they admit a weakness.

"My job is to help you figure out why this is happening. And once we know *why* it's happening, we can put an end to it. And once we do that, the sky is the limit.

"Look at me, Bobby."

I looked up and saw Wally's eyes of certainty.

"There's no reason you couldn't be back in the majors by the end of this summer," he said. "I know you don't believe that right now. But we're going to change your beliefs."

7

Wally was behind the wheel, driving us to Springfield, Missouri, where we would play against the Springfield Cardinals (St. Louis' Double-A affiliate). That meant an easy road trip of just over two hours. Riding in a comfy RV and listening to a baseball guy talk like I'd never heard a baseball guy talk before, I found myself wishing—for the first time in my career—that a road trip would last *longer*.

Wally gave me a black notebook small enough to fit in my back pocket. He said he wanted me to write down some things he was going to teach me.

"Call it, *Wally's Little Black Book of Wisdom*," he said with a smile.

"The first thing you have to understand is the power of your mindset," Wally said as we cruised down the highway. "That's the first lesson. Write this down: **Your mind is the most powerful weapon you have. It affects everything.** *Everything.*

"This is hard for a lot of guys to understand. They spend hours in the weight room, hours in the batting cage, hours watching film and breaking down every little physical detail, but they never spend any time working on their most important muscle: their mind.

"Organizations are finally understanding how important this mindset stuff is. The big-league teams now hire sports psychologists and peak-performance coaches. But they can't afford those experts at the lower levels of play. Trainers, strength and conditioning coaches, sure, but you won't find any mindset coaches in Double-A ball. And that's what most guys need, *especially* at this level."

I wrote down what Wally told me to write down and I enjoyed listening to him. But, I was skeptical of what he was saying. He must have sensed that.

"You think I'm full of crap, don't you?" Wally said.

"I've heard all this positive thinking stuff before," I said. "I have a hard time buying into it. Remember, I'm not exactly a rookie. I used to be that glass-half-full kind of guy, but I've been in this business for thirteen *long* years. I've seen enough to know what works and what doesn't.

"The truth is, pure dumb luck plays a much bigger role than anyone wants to admit. The difference between a guy getting called up or sent down can be less than four or five hits over the course of two months, one ump's bad strike zone, just being in the right place at the right time when someone above you sprains his ankle. If it was really as easy as you say — just have a positive attitude and everything will work out fine — everybody would be doing it and getting instant results."

"I never said it was easy." Wally smiled. "You sound like me when I first heard about the power of optimism. I totally blew it off. Thought it was all Pollyanna B.S.

"You see, when I started out, I was one of those scrappy players with a chip on my shoulder, always trying to prove myself by being the most aggressive guy in the ballpark. That's what got me in the door. That's what got me signed to play professional baseball in the first place.

"But I was all brawn and no brains. I thought I could muscle through every problem. I soon realized that everybody on a minor league roster is an outstanding player from wherever they came from. Anybody getting *paid* to play baseball has proven that he's one of the best ballplayers in the world. *Everybody* here has talent. Lots of talent. The difference between playing Double-A, Triple-A, or in the majors really *is* razor-thin when it comes to talent.

"After five years in the minors and failing to climb above A-ball, I went searching for an edge," Wally continued. "I wanted to know what separated the guys who made it from the guys who didn't. If talent alone wasn't enough—since it was so close to being equal for the vast majority of players at this level—I wanted to find the thing that *did* put guys over the top.

"I needed that edge or else I wouldn't make it; I knew that for sure. I had natural talent. I had the work ethic and the athletic skills to be one of the best ballplayers my little hometown had ever produced. But *everybody* in the minors can tell that story. I wanted to separate myself from all the other talented guys I was playing with. I wanted to find the difference-maker and use it."

Wally knew how to intrigue me. He made it sound like he had gone searching for some hidden treasure.

"The first thing I noticed was that some guys cruised into professional baseball with natural talent, but a poor work ethic," Wally said. "Those guys were exposed quickly. They either learned how to work hard or they were shown the door. Most never lasted more than a couple years in the minors before their teams cut 'em loose.

"That left the rest of us. Those who were talented, but also passionate enough about baseball to work our butts off to become better ballplayers. Out of this group, which is most the people who stick around for any worthwhile amount of time, I wanted to find that edge that made up for the razor-thin difference between life in the minors and big-time contracts in the majors."

"And you found it?" I asked.

"I did. **Talent and hard work will get you in the door, but it's your mindset — your attitude — that will take you to the top.** Do me a favor and write that down."

I did as he asked.

"Once I realized the power of my mindset, everything changed for me," Wally said. "But, like you, it was hard for me to buy into at first. And that's what I'm here for — to help you see just how powerful the mental side of this game is. How important the mental side is for baseball and for every other area of your life. Like Yogi Berra used to say, 'Baseball is 90 percent mental, the other half is physical.' There's a lot of truth to that famous statement."

I could hear the sincerity in Wally's voice. And he didn't come across like some cheesy positive-thinking guru like you might see on TV infomercials late at night. He was a man's man. He was an old-school ballplayer through and through. He was the very opposite of the "I'm-okay-you're-okay" Stuart Smalley-type self-help people.

Wally believed what he was saying. With all his heart, he *believed* it.

But still, I wasn't ready to take that leap.

"Look, I know it's important to have a positive attitude and all that," I said. "But I tried it. I used to be the most positive guy on the team and it never got me anywhere. Sure, I'd rather be positive than negative, happy instead of depressed, who wouldn't? I just think all that positive attitude stuff is way overblown."

"It's not," Wally said. "In fact, it doesn't get nearly the attention it should. Not by a long shot. My personal experience confirms how powerful a man's mindset is. I've got three World Series rings to prove it."

My head snapped toward Wally. "Three?"

"Three—and I never played for the Yankees," Wally said proudly. "I got my first ring with the '85 Royals. I got traded to the Mets the next season and we won it all in '86. In 1988, I signed with the Dodgers and Tommy Lasorda, the greatest manager I've ever known, led us to a championship that year."

"You won three rings with three different teams in four seasons?" I said. "You're like the luckiest guy in the history of baseball."

"I won't deny that," Wally said with a big smile. "Once I changed my mindset, my *luck* changed too. I'm living proof this stuff works."

"I have to admit, now you've got my attention," I said. "But you know what I think? I think we all tend to remember things differently in hindsight. We remember how positive and happy we were once we were winning, but we confuse the cause with the effect. I get happy and positive when I'm playing well, and I get negative when I'm in a slump. Everybody does. That's the way life goes. Once I start seeing results, *then* I'll get all positive and cheery."

"That's where you're wrong," Wally said. "My luck changed *after* I consciously changed my attitude. I made the effort to change my thinking and the outcomes I experienced followed this change.

"Don't just take my word for it. I didn't take any one man's word for it either. I spent an offseason in the library researching this stuff and found that there's plenty of science to back it up. **Success *follows* optimism; it's not the other way around. A positive attitude delivers positive outcomes.** *In everything.*

"Study after study shows that people who have an optimistic attitude live longer, they're healthier, they're less stressed, they're more successful in their careers, they have happier marriages, they make more money, they're more energetic, they have more meaningful relationships, and they report being much happier than the rest of the population. In other words, optimistic people are healthier, wealthier, happier, and a hell of a lot more fun to be around than everyone else.

"Don't believe me? I've got a few books for you to read with all the science that backs this stuff up. Grab that bag sitting on the couch in the back, will ya?"

I walked to the back of the RV and picked up a shopping bag that contained a handful of books.

"Those are my gift to you," Wally yelled from the front seat. "It's also your summer reading assignment."

I thumbed through the titles. There were five books: *Learned Optimism*, *The Happiness Advantage*, *The Magic of Thinking Big*, *How Champions Think*, and *Psycho-Cybernetics*. I noticed each book was written by a doctor and I picked up on the theme quickly.

"*Psycho-Cybernetics*?" I asked as I returned to the front passenger seat with the book in my hand. "Never heard of it."

"That book's an old one," Wally said. "It came out in the sixties, but still holds up. Vince Lombardi was a big fan of it. He had the Packers read it—Bart Starr, Jerry Kramer, those NFL legends."

"Thanks, Wally," I said. "I really appreciate you taking an interest in me—I really do—but I gotta be honest, I'm not much of a reader."

"Consider it mandatory gym time," Wally said almost before I finished my sentence. He'd obviously heard my excuse many times in the past.

"It's like weight lifting for your mind," Wally said. "You need it just as much as you need physical weight lifting.

"**Nothing is more important than what you feed your mind.** Write that down. **And the best way to**

feed your mind is with the books you read."

"If you say so," I said with a condescending tone.

"This isn't a joke," Wally snapped, for the first time showing impatience with my snarkiness.

"Let me make this clear," Wally continued, this time pointing a finger at me. "**Success begins in your mind. But failure does too. Optimism is self-fulfilling, but so is pessimism. You have to decide how you're going to think. The choice is yours and you have to own the outcome.**

"Do you want to make your dreams come true, or not?" he asked.

"Of course, I do," I said.

"Then do what I'm asking. Cut the cynical crap and drop the skepticism. Commit to this for one summer. If you're not seeing real results on the field and in your personal life, then forget everything I'm saying.

"What do you have to lose? You're not where you want to be. What you've been doing hasn't been working for you. You can go on doing what you've been doing and hope for different results or you can have the courage to question your beliefs and think differently.

"Commit to what I'm saying for the summer.

That's all I'm asking. I can't *make* you change your thinking. You have to make the commitment. All I'm asking is that for as long as you're here you drop the pessimism and give it a shot. Deal?"

Wally held out his hand and I shook his firm grip.

8

Our three-game series against the Springfield Cardinals was my best stretch since the previous summer. I smacked two home runs—my first of the season—and ended up batting .500 for the series.

As Wally had asked me to do, I started skimming some of the books he'd given me. I had to admit, they made a compelling case for this positive thinking stuff, but I was sure that the sudden change in my performance on the field was because Wally had helped me fix my swing mechanics—not because I was reading self-improvement books. I made a disciplined effort to keep my head from drifting upward and the adjustment was paying off instantly, just as Wally had promised it would.

Though I may not have been buying into everything Wally was saying about the power of your mind, I had no doubt this guy knew baseball and he had a sharp eye for what needed to be fixed.

Still, I wasn't *completely* blowing off all the mindset stuff Wally was trying to teach me. I started wondering, *What if Wally is right? What if it wasn't the so-called baseball gods who were holding my career back, but what if I was sabotaging myself with my own attitude? What if I was doing this subconsciously?*

I wanted to get an objective opinion on this, so I called Janey.

Nowadays, it seemed like she always answered the phone with a frantic, "Is everything okay?" Every time she saw my number calling, she must have wondered if this was the call telling her I'd been released and my career was over. Once I assured her I was still employed in the minors, her voice always shifted to a quick *then why are you calling me?* tone.

This was so unlike the upbeat Janey I used to always call from the road. The years of struggle and disappointment had changed her, just as it had changed me.

"I've got a strange question for you and I want you to be completely honest with me," I said after asking how the kids were doing. "Over these past ten years, I know I've been a little more…negative at times."

"You think?" she said sarcastically, but just playful enough to give me a glimpse of the good times and fun conversations we used to regularly have. How I missed the way things used to be with us.

"I know I haven't been easy to be around, especially in recent months," I said, trying not to get sidetracked. "But can you tell me, can you think back hard and tell me, honestly, did my attitude turn more negative *before* I started struggling on the field or after?"

"Is this a trick question?" she asked.

"No, I seriously want to know."

"When you started out you were so optimistic about our future. You and I used to talk about our dreams with so much hope. When Boston traded you, I think that's when it began. That's when you started sliding, becoming less hopeful about the future, angry at the Red Sox."

"So it was *after* the wrist injury, right?" I asked.

"Yes. That was a wake-up call for both of us. We realized this wasn't going to be the fairy-tale life we had imagined."

"*After* the injury and *after* the trade from Boston; that's when it happened, right?"

"Of course," Janey said, a little irritated now. "Why would you have been unhappy *before* the bad news?"

"You're right, that's what I thought. I just wanted

to be sure."

"Glad I could help. Look, I've got to run. Travel safe and play hard."

It wasn't much, but Janey's signoff was the first words of encouragement she'd offered me since this season had begun. I don't know what caused it, but I was glad to hear it.

More importantly, Janey confirmed exactly what I had told Wally on the trip to Springfield. My negative attitude had been a *response* to my negative results; it wasn't the *cause* of them.

There were just too many holes in all this positive thinking stuff.

9

To the dismay of my teammates, I was once again invited to ride with Wally for our next road trip — this time a four-hour trip to Little Rock, Arkansas.

"You've got to be feeling great after the way you were swinging the bat this weekend," Wally said about thirty minutes into our trip.

"You're right," I said. "I am feeling great. And those great feelings came along *after* I started hitting home runs again."

"Funny how that works, isn't it?" Wally said.

"Yes, and it confirms exactly what I was saying the last time we were on this bus. We all tend to *think positive* after things start going well." As I said *think positive* I made air quotes with my fingers. "But the positive thoughts come along *after* the results, not before. People look back on good times, remember how good they felt, and they confuse the cause with the effect.

"I've been thinking a lot about what you said and also reflecting on my career. I even called my wife to make sure I was remembering things correctly. I confirmed that I had no trouble being the optimistic guy early in my career, right up until I injured my wrist and lost my spot with the Red Sox. That's when I first took off my rose-colored glasses. It was *after* a negative event, not before. The event caused an attitude shift; attitude didn't cause the event."

"Let me stop you right there and get something straight," Wally said. "I know when some people talk about *positive thinking*, they make it sound like if you just think positive thoughts everything will be okay and nothing will ever go wrong." Wally mocked my air quotes with his own as he emphasized the words, *positive thinking*. "But that's *not* how positive thinking works. That's certainly not what I'm talking about when I talk about optimism.

"That's *wishful* thinking, not positive thinking. There's a huge difference between the two."

"Let me stop *you* right there," I said proudly, as though I'd backed my wannabe-mentor into a corner. "Four days ago you sat in that chair and told me that positive thinking leads to positive results. You said a positive attitude was the cause and not the effect."

"Actually," Wally interrupted. "I said that positive

thinking leads to positive *outcomes*, which I believe is a key difference. Most people tend to think of results in the short-term and outcomes in the long-term. The *results* of a single baseball game as opposed to the *outcome* of a baseball season or a baseball career, for example. Wouldn't you agree?"

"I guess, but call it whatever you want, we're still talking about causes versus effects."

"Fair enough," Wally shrugged. "I just want to make it clear that there's a big difference between short-term results and long-term outcomes." He didn't seem irritated by my argumentative tone. He seemed to like that I was giving his teachings thoughtful consideration and was eager to get into a more meaningful conversation.

"Grab your notebook, this is important," Wally said. I did as I was told, though I sighed as I did it.

"**Failure and negative events are a part of life**," he said. "**There's nothing you can do to protect yourself from encountering adversity. Anybody who thinks they can is delusional and only setting themselves up for a lifetime of disappointment.**

"There are a lot of people in the positive thinking movement who promote something closer to *magical* thinking. They sell you on the false promise that if you just have a positive attitude, nothing bad will ever happen to you. That's simply not true. You can be the most positive person there is and you're still going to stub your toe, have losing streaks, get sick, and lose loved ones. No matter how optimistic you are, bad things are going to happen to you sometimes.

"Here's the key: **Optimism won't prevent negative events from happening; optimism will ensure that you *respond* to those negative events in the most beneficial way possible—a way that leads to positive outcomes. Your mindset determines how you *respond* to the negative events that will inevitably happen to us all.**"

I had to concede, this was a different point of view than what I always believed people meant when they talked about positive thinking.

"When a negative event happens, you're given a choice," Wally continued. "**You can respond with pessimism or you can respond with optimism. Those who respond with pessimism—most people—will bring about more problems and, ultimately, negative outcomes. Those who respond with optimism will turn the negative situation around and ensure a positive outcome in the long run.**

"Baseball is the perfect example of all this. It's a sport of *failure*. Think about it, the very best batters in the world are those with a batting average above .300 at the end of the year. That means that the best hitters in all of baseball—the *very* best—still fail seven out of every ten times they step up to the plate. We get so impressed by someone who achieves a .300 batting average over a long stretch that we forget we're still talking about a guy who fails *seventy* percent of the time!

"In 1928, Ty Cobb retired with history's highest career batting average. He batted .366 over his career. Nobody has come close to matching his batting average in the modern era of baseball because pitchers are so much better now — they get proper rest between outings and they aren't wearing out their arms every other night. And yet, even back then, Ty Cobb failed more than sixty-three percent of the time. Ted Williams failed sixty-six percent of the time, so did Babe Ruth and Tony Gwynn. Stan Musial and Wade Boggs failed sixty-seven percent of the time. You get my point. We're talking about the greatest batters in the history of baseball and they all *failed* roughly twice as often as they succeeded. That's an awful lot of failure. That's an awful lot of negative results to deal with. And we're talking about the greatest ballplayers ever.

"Same thing for teams. The best team in baseball each year, the team that wins the World Series will usually lose sixty games or more during the season. *Sixty* losses for the best team in the world. That's an awful lot of failure to endure. No other team sport comes close to breaking your heart this often."

"It's a cruel sport," I said.

"It's a beautiful sport," Wally corrected. "It's an honest sport. It teaches you exactly what you need to know about life: **the people who succeed aren't the ones who avoid failure; they're the ones who learn how to respond to failure with optimism**.

"Everyone encounters negative events — a strikeout at the plate, a bad break at work, a lost job, a bad grade, whatever. And most people respond to those negative events with a pessimistic response.

"They react by telling themselves that the negative event is permanent. They convince themselves that they missed their chance at success — that this disappointment is the first of many more to come and that new or better opportunities will never come again.

"They tell themselves that the negative event is contagious. They think it will lead to negative events in other areas of life. They worry that because one thing went wrong now *everything* is going to go wrong.

"And finally, they make the negative event personal. They beat themselves up and think the negative result is all their fault. They didn't just experience a failure; they convince themselves that they've *become* failures."

"Maybe it *is* their fault," I said. "I've always been taught that you should take personal responsibility for your failures. What about owning your results?"

"You should…to a point," Wally said. "You have to do everything you can to put yourself in a position to succeed. You have to put in the work, both physical and mental, and you have to take total responsibility for how well prepared you are. Those are things you have control over. If you don't put in the work necessary or if there's something you should have done differently, then you absolutely have to own that and correct your mistakes.

"But, you also have to recognize that you don't

have control over *everything*. Nobody does. Some days the pitcher you're facing is going to throw an amazing game. He gets so hot that nobody is able to hit off of him. You can't beat yourself up over that outing and let it affect your next game. A guy can be the best employee he can possibly be, but if he loses his job because the company gets bought out or the factory gets shut down, he can't beat himself up over something that was completely out of his control. If he does, he'll convince himself that he deserved to be fired and doesn't deserve another job.

"I'm all for taking personal responsibility and learning from mistakes, but you can't be naïve about it. There are some things out of your control and you have to accept that as part of life. If you don't, you'll be lying to yourself and setting yourself up for failure in the future. Know what I mean?"

I nodded my head. He made a good point.

"Okay," I said, "If most people tell themselves that a negative event is permanent, contagious, and personal, how do optimists respond to those same negative events? What do they do differently?"

"I'm glad you asked." Wally pointed to my notebook. "This is important."

"Optimists remind themselves that every negative event is a lie. That's capital L-I-E.

"**The L stands for Limited. Optimists see the negative event as temporary and limited to a single moment.** A strikeout was a failure in that particular at-bat, but it's over and done with. You have to move on. It has nothing to do with what will happen the next time you're up to bat—except that it's a good learning opportunity for having a better outing next time.

"**The I is for Isolated. Optimists see the negative event as specific to that one particular area.** It isn't contagious and it won't spread to anything else…if you don't let it. A failure at the plate should have nothing to do with how you play defensively the rest of the game. Along those same lines, there's no reason to let a negative event at work affect your health or your family life. Yet, most people do. It's all in their mind.

"**The E is for External. Optimists remind themselves that people and things outside of their control contributed to the negative event.** Failure is external, not internal. Don't let a single negative event become personal and affect your self-worth. A slump on the baseball field does not mean *you're* a failure; it means you've encountered a negative event and now you have the chance to respond positively to it."

Everything Wally was saying *not* to do when you encounter a negative event is exactly what I had been doing for most of the past ten years.

"Remember that," Wally said. "**Failure is a lie; that's L-I-E. Failure is Limited, Isolated, and External. It's Limited to one particular moment, it's Isolated to one particular area, and it occurred Externally—outside of you.**"

With the type of urgency you feel when you learn something new and exciting, I wrote down the words Wally was saying as fast as I could.

"You see," Wally continued. "We're not talking about positive vibes and happy feelings here. That's not what optimism is. We're talking about logic.

"When people experience negative events, they usually lie to themselves. You have to recognize those *LIEs* and stop them in their tracks. Very few people get this. They feed themselves pessimistic lies after each setback and it creates a vicious cycle of new setbacks— in future events, in other areas of their life, and deep inside of them. It drags them down and whittles away at their self-esteem."

Sitting in that RV, looking out the window and watching the clouds roll by on a beautiful spring morning, something clicked inside me. I don't know quite how to explain it other than that it was one of those rare moments in life where you feel yourself changing. You suddenly see things you could not see before.

No one had ever talked to me about how to deal with adversity this way. I'd never really thought about it this specifically. I didn't pay all that much attention to the thoughts in my head and what I might be telling myself in response to setbacks.

Now, I could see it. I *had* been sabotaging myself. I *was* making things worse.

But could it really be that simple?

Recognizing what I was doing to myself was only the first step — an important one, for sure — but it also led to a very important question. A question that needed an honest answer.

10

"You may be right about all this," I said. "I'm guilty of doing the things you're talking about. But it brings up an important question."

"It brings up a lot of important questions," Wally said. "That's what I'm here for."

"The idea that a negative event is a lie—L.I.E.— sounds great, but experience tells me otherwise." I said. "Usually, failures and setbacks *do* have a domino effect that leads to more failures. It's called a slump and we all have them.

"Most the time in my life, failure *is* contagious and leads to problems in other areas. When I fail on the baseball field, it impacts my income and my family feels it too.

"A lot of times I beat myself up after a setback because it *was* my fault and I deserve it.

"How do you know you're right and I'm wrong? How do you know you're not being delusional by claiming a setback is a LIE? How can you prove that the negative event is, in fact, a LIE?"

Wally nodded and pointed at my notebook, indicating that what he was about to say was something I needed to write down.

"**It's only a lie — L.I.E. — if *you* make it so**," Wally said. "**That's the key. Whether you view a negative event as a pessimist and allow it to fester and make things worse or whether you view it as an optimist and define it as a LIE — something Limited, Isolated, and External — that will not lead to further damage is completely up to you. *You* have the power.**

"*That* is what optimism is all about. *That* is what I mean when I say that your thoughts determine your outcomes. You have control over this.

"A setback *will* create a domino effect if you tell yourself this is the first of many negative events to come.

"Failure *will* be contagious if you get down on yourself and carry a negative attitude into other areas of your life because of this one thing that went wrong.

"You *will* feel bad about yourself and make things much worse if you beat yourself up when things don't go your way even though you gave it your best.

"But it's all up to you. **You — and only you — control your thoughts. And how you choose to**

respond to a negative event will determine your outcome."

"If that's the case," I said, "If we're all sabotaging ourselves with pessimistic thinking, why did any of us start thinking this way in the first place? If our minds are so powerful, where did this pessimistic way of thinking come from? If it only leads to more failure, shouldn't our minds have stopped these LIEs before they ever got started?"

"You nailed it," Wally smacked the steering wheel in victory, as if his pitcher had just struck out the final batter of the night. **"The mind's natural state is optimism. It's designed to be a success-seeking, can-do, positive-thinking mechanism. We're all wired to be successful.** Your mind naturally seeks to tell you the truth, which is that negative events are only temporary, they're not contagious, and they're not internal. Your mind naturally seeks to solve problems quickly. It naturally seeks to achieve the biggest dreams you give it.

"Think of kids. Think of how quickly they bounce back up when learning to walk or falling off a bike. Think of how quickly they rebound from disappointments. Think of how big their dreams are;

they want to be presidents, doctors, leaders, and professional ballplayers. Yet, as they grow older, what happens to that attitude? What happens to those big dreams?"

"They grow up and realize they have to be more realistic." I said. "They learn how the world works, right?"

"Wrong," Wally said. "They learn how *other people* tell them the world works. And they start accepting the lies they are told. Some coach tells them they're not talented enough to chase their dream. Some teacher tells them they're not smart enough. Well-meaning parents tell them their ambitions are too high and they're setting themselves up for disappointment. So-called *friends* convince them that big dreams rarely come true. People convince them it's all one big lottery and that success is based on random luck. These kids get convinced by others that big goals aren't worth the effort and that they're better off not trying at all.

"Soon, they start responding to negative events differently. Negative events that they would have shrugged off quickly—*if* they had maintained an optimistic attitude—now crush their spirits and confirm the pessimistic viewpoints they've been taught by others.

"Slowly, but surely, people change their thinking due to all these outside influences. They *learn* to be cynical, to *expect* disappointment, and to *become* pessimists.

"And, because most of us never pay much attention to the thoughts we think, how we're talking to ourselves, and how we're actually responding to the events we encounter; we accept this pessimistic attitude and figure that's just the way it is. We never stop to evaluate if what we're telling ourselves is actually true.

"Little do we know, we're sabotaging ourselves; we're setting ourselves up for more failure."

As Wally spoke, memories from my past flashed through my mind. I thought about words that were said to me growing up and the words of a long-ago coach who told me if I didn't make it to the majors by the age of 30 I had no chance. I thought about how I was accepting these beliefs. *Why? What did these people really know about me? Why was I letting their beliefs affect my beliefs?*

Wally was right. As people grow older, most of us *do* turn into pessimists.

"All these negative beliefs you've been taught prevent your mind from doing its job," Wally said. "It's like your mind is a computer that gets reprogrammed with negative software, negative thinking. And that ensures negative outcomes.

"You want to know what your life will look like a year from now? Listen to what you're saying when you talk to yourself. Your self-talk determines your future."

Wally was silent for a stretch of highway, letting me take in what he was saying.

"I think you're convincing me," I blurted out.

My concession surprised me and it seemed to surprise Wally too as he looked my way to make sure I wasn't being sarcastic.

"Yeah?" he asked.

"Yes." I was shaking my head as I thought about it. "I see it. I see how it's happened to me. I'm not completely convinced that my thinking was the cause of it all, but I do see a possible connection in hindsight. Everything you're saying—the negative self-talk, the negative beliefs—I'm guilty of it.

"Maybe it's out of desperation, but I'm willing to give your way a shot. I'll try anything to get back on track."

"Sometimes it takes desperation to force us to make positive changes in our lives," Wally said.

"So, now what? How do I reverse the damage? If years of negative programming have changed my thinking, will it take me years to get back to the way I *should* be thinking?"

11

"How quickly you change your mindset is up to you," Wally said. "But I won't sugarcoat it. It's not going to be instant. It's not as simple as, 'Think happy thoughts and all your problems will melt away.' It's going to take a lot of discipline on your part."

"I understand," I said. "Whatever it takes. I want the edge back. I had it when I was younger. I lost it. I need to find it again."

"And you will," Wally said. "If you *commit* to the techniques I'm going to teach you. **Anyone can be an optimist for a day, a week, maybe a few months when things are going well.** It's especially easier when you're younger. But eventually, adversity will strike again. It always does. **It's a *commitment* to long-term positive thinking that separates the big achievers from everyone else.**"

I nodded. "I'll do it."

"I'm glad to hear that. The first thing you need to do is start monitoring your self-talk. Beginning with tonight's game, I want you to pay attention to what you're saying when you talk to yourself. Most people never pay attention to their inner dialogue, but it's that inner dialogue that determines your destiny.

"This isn't as easy as it sounds. Monitoring the thoughts that pop into your head can be exhausting, especially at first. I don't want you to drive yourself crazy with it.

"So, just focus on the important moments. Being a ballplayer makes this easier. I want you monitoring your thoughts after each at-bat, whether the at-bat was good or bad. What are you saying to yourself as you walk back to the dugout after a strikeout and what are you saying to yourself as you round third after hitting a dinger into the bleachers?

"As you evaluate yourself, I think you'll discover how remarkably consistent your self-talk is — though that's not necessarily a good thing if you're consistently negative."

"Why be so concerned with what I'm saying to myself after a *good* at-bat?" I asked. "Of course I'm going to be happy and feeling good after hitting a home run. If optimism is all about how you respond to negative events, what's the point of scrutinizing the positive events? Why not just embrace the good feelings and be grateful for them?"

"What I think you'll find is that your response to positive events is not as optimistic as you might assume. **How you respond to positive events is just as important as how you respond to negative events.** Trust me on this.

"After each game, I want you to sit down, reflect honestly on the night, and write down what you were saying to yourself following each at-bat. Same thing after key defensive plays. If a line drive slips past you, what are you saying to yourself? If you rob a home run, what are you thinking then?

"The big moments," Wally stressed. "Don't worry about monitoring every single thought because it'll lock you up and take you out of the present. I want you monitoring your self-talk after the key moments throughout the game.

"**Optimism starts with becoming aware of your thoughts and beliefs. You have to clearly identify your fears, worries, and other negative thoughts before you can overcome them.**"

"Then what?" I asked. "Once I recognize them, then what do I do?"

"Then, you start arguing with them," Wally said.

12

Our first game against the Arkansas Travelers was a good opportunity to do exactly what Wally had asked me to do. The Travelers had one of the best up-and-coming pitchers in Double-A, a 20-year-old from the Dominican Republic named Carlos Martinez. He was a first-round draft pick for the Seattle Mariners and the kid had serious heat. He'd already been clocked at 101 miles-per-hour, but he was more than a fastball alone; he could also throw breaking balls that made some of the best young hitters look ridiculous. Just a few months into his first Double-A season, Martinez was already the talk of the Texas League.

I kept track of my self-talk as best as I could throughout the night and when I got back to my hotel room after the game, I pulled out my notebook and recorded those thoughts.

Here's what I wrote:

First inning at-bat. Struck out chasing a curveball by Martinez. I expected this kid to rely on his fastball early and I paid the price for guessing wrong.

SELF-TALK: "You've been in this league for thirteen years and this rookie just made you look stupid. You ARE stupid when you play like that. You're ALWAYS trying to guess what's coming next, thinking you're smarter than everyone, and you're ALWAYS wrong."

EVALUATION: First, I made it personal. *I internalized the negative event and told myself I was stupid because of it. I should've recognized that this was one of the hottest young pitchers in baseball and this was my first time ever facing him. The Mariners wouldn't have given this kid a multimillion-dollar contract if he didn't know what he was doing. I also made it* permanent. *I don't ALWAYS guess wrong; I've had nearly 200 home runs throughout my professional career to prove that I'm often correct.*

Third inning at-bat. *Popped up for an easy out. Got underneath Martinez's fastball.*

SELF-TALK: "Missed a perfect *opportunity to go deep on this kid. Man, I want that one back...* bad. *He probably knows not to throw the high fastball at me again and I doubt I'll ever see another perfect setup like that from him."*

EVALUATION: Once again, I immediately made my mistake permanent *in my mind. I was mad at myself for missing a golden opportunity, but I didn't need to tell myself that I would never see that pitch again. I should've told myself I WOULD get a pitch like that again...and next time I'd be ready.*

Fourth inning double-play. I was moved in from the outfield and playing first base tonight. It had been awhile since I'd played first and during this particular play I had to stretch out and snag a wild throw from our shortstop to complete a double-play and end the inning.

SELF-TALK: "Great job! Shows these guys that an old man like me still has some athleticism."

EVALUATION: Happy with myself for making the play, but why did I call myself an "old man?" I work out harder than anybody in order to stay in shape, extend my career, and continue making plays like that.

Fifth inning at-bat. Martinez started showing some signs of fatigue, but I hit a grounder to third and was thrown out at first. I left two of our guys on base to end the inning.

SELF-TALK: "So much for being a good athlete. You were thrown out way too easily, Bobby. There's no room in the majors for a guy as slow as you. It's plays like that that are letting Janey and the kids down."

EVALUATION: Wow, way too negative here. First off, there are plenty of slow guys in the majors who are there for their power. Secondly, I may not be the fastest guy on the team, but I'm definitely not slow. In fact, I'm sure I place in the upper half of the team as far as speed goes. The problem on this play was with my grounder, not my speed. Very few — if any — major-leaguers could've beat that throw. And why did I make this about Janey and the kids? It was ONE play in the stat sheet and had little to no effect on my salary or my family back in Massachusetts.

Seventh inning at-bat. I struck out swinging in my last time facing Martinez.

SELF-TALK: *"You thought he was running out of gas, but he showed you. This time he went low on you, made you look like a fool hoping for the high fastball again."*

EVALUATION: *Again, why did I make this personal? This Martinez kid is the real deal. He pitched seven scoreless innings tonight. I'll get a chance to face him again.*

Ninth inning at-bat. After Martinez left the game, we rallied and I stepped up to the plate with the bases loaded in the ninth. I swung at the first pitch and sent it over the right field wall for my first grand slam of the year. It gave us the lead, a lead we held onto for the win tonight.

SELF-TALK: *"That felt great! I only wish it had come against Martinez. That would've shown the organization something. As it is, my slam came against a guy that was already rattled. I caught him on a bad night."*

EVALUATION: *I have no problem making it personal and blaming myself when I fail, but yet I can't make it personal and give myself credit when I succeed? That's pretty messed up. I beat myself up for failing against Martinez, but when I hit a grand slam off of their closer, I give HIM the credit for throwing me an easy pitch?*

How revealing these notes were.

First, I was quickly realizing just how negative my self-talk was following negative events.

But, I was also surprised to see how negative my self-talk was after *positive* events. I now understood why Wally wanted me to monitor my self-talk after both negative and positive moments.

13

After my self-evaluation exercise, I felt like a scientist who had just made an important discovery. I couldn't wait to show Wally my results and discuss my findings. I went out to the hotel parking lot and knocked on his RV door.

"One second," Wally said from inside.

I heard muffled talking and walked back twenty feet or so, not wanting to seem like I was eavesdropping. A minute or two later, the door opened and out walked one of my teammates, rubbing his misty eyes and smiling. He gave me a nod and then shook his head.

"Man, that dude is like a shrink or something," he said to me. "He knows things about me I never knew about myself."

I laughed. "I know exactly what you mean."

It was after midnight, but Wally warmly welcomed me into his RV, his bus, his office on wheels, whatever you want to call it.

"I hope it's not too late," I said.

"Not at all, I'm a night owl and my door is always open to my players," Wally said. "This is when some of the best coaching is done, when the emotions of the game are still fresh."

I shook my head with a chuckle and repeated what had become a common thought for me, "Wally, you're not like any manager I've ever had."

"I'll take that as a good thing. **Doing things the way everybody else does them is the surest road to mediocrity.** What did you want to talk about?"

"I want to show you my results," I said as I handed him my notebook.

"You sure you want me to read this?" Wally asked. "This is personal and you need to know that you can be completely honest with yourself without worrying about what I — or anyone else — might think."

"Good to know for the future, but there's nothing in there that's too personal. I *want* you to read it."

Wally took a couple minutes to read the entries I had written down earlier in the night. When he finished, he looked up at me with a twinkle in his eye and a half-grin on his face.

"You see it, don't you?" he asked.

"It's kind of hard to miss it. Whether something

bad *or* good happens, I'm feeding myself negativity."

Wally nodded. "This is very common. This is how most people talk to themselves. We do this without even realizing it."

"So, what's the next step? Now that I know how pessimistic I am, what do I do to turn it around?"

"First off, you're doing it again right now. You're making a mistake personal and permanent: saying, 'how pessimistic *I am.*'

"*You're* not pessimistic, your *thoughts* have been pessimistic and you can change that.

"How are you going to do that? By doing exactly what you did in this notebook.

"The way you argued with your negative thoughts in this notebook is exactly what you need to do in real-time, as soon as you hear negative thoughts. **Recognize the negative thought, remind yourself that it's a LIE — Limited, Isolated, and External — and then explain to yourself exactly *why* it's a lie.** Just like you did in your self-evaluation tonight."

"That's it? I don't need to be hypnotized or anything?" I asked with a smile.

"That's it. Be aware of what you're saying, then counter the negative self-talk with positive self-talk.

You started doing it in these entries, when you had a chance to evaluate yourself with honesty. Now, you have to start doing it right as it happens.

"It's a quick three-step process. You have to get in the habit of instantly *recognizing* those negative thoughts, *arguing* with the LIEs they try to tell, and then *replacing* those negative thoughts with positive thoughts.

"Recognize. Argue. Replace.

"Once you realize you've made a negative event personal, for example, you have to remind yourself that it's the other way around. *You* **aren't a failure because you experienced a failure. You're a successful person who temporarily failed and is now returning to your natural state of success.**

"If you're telling yourself that a mistake is contagious and spreading to other things, zap that LIE immediately. A mistake in baseball has nothing whatsoever to do with what kind of husband you are, what kind of father you can be, how healthy you are, what you should be feeling later tonight, or what kind of person you're becoming. **A negative event is a single isolated event that you can stop in its tracks and make sure it will never affect you — or anything else in your life — again.**

"If you've made a negative result permanent in your mind, turn it around quickly. **You didn't miss out on your *only* shot at success. That negative experience will now lead to positive experiences in the future because it has made you smarter and more prepared for the future. You're now wiser, more experienced, and one step closer to the inevitable success you've prepared yourself for.**

"See what I'm doing here? You have to quickly counter those negative thoughts with positive thoughts."

"I think I can do that," I said.

"I *know* you can. And every time you do it, you're going to be slowly reprogramming your mindset. Soon, it will be a habit and you'll naturally be responding to negative events with positive self-talk.

"How do I know this? Because, like I said before, optimism is your mind's natural state and it *wants* to accept the can-do attitude it was made for.

"But, also like I told you before, it's going to take a lot of commitment and discipline on your part. It won't happen overnight.

"Are you committed to making this change?"

"I'm committed," I said.

When I left Wally's office on wheels, I saw Ricky Alvarez sitting at the hotel door reading a familiar-looking book—one of the books Wally had given to me as well.

He hopped up when he saw me and asked, "Wally still up?"

I nodded.

"What do you think of all this stuff he's preaching, Bobby?" Ricky asked.

"I'm thinking, I wish somebody had taught me this stuff when I was as young as you are."

That night, I went to bed excited about tomorrow. For the first time in months, I was *optimistic* about my future.

14

I would come to believe that Wally wasn't wrong about much, but as May turned to June it became abundantly clear that he was very wrong about one thing. He told me not to expect instant results with this new way of thinking. He said it would take some time to change my mindset and start seeing positive results (or, positive *outcomes*, as he liked to clarify).

Yet, following my declaration that I was now *committed* to this new way of thinking, I instantly got on the hottest hot streak of my career.

Over a ten-game stretch, I hit nine home runs—*nine!*—while batting over .400. Just ridiculous numbers. I was seeing every pitch from the moment it left the pitcher's hand and when I guessed on an upcoming pitch, I guessed right more often than not. When I wasn't hitting dingers, I was ripping unplayable shots just inside the foul line.

Even when I didn't connect well, the ball fell my way. In one at-bat against the Arkansas Travelers, I broke my bat, which is usually an easy out. Instead, the ball did what you'd hope to do with a perfectly-placed bunt and settled in that no-man's-land near the third base line where neither the third baseman, the catcher, nor the pitcher had a fast path to it. I was safe at first by a mile. It was almost inexplicable the kind of luck I was having.

And *that sound*, a sound I used to hear often, *that sound* that got me labeled a hot prospect ten years ago, *that sound* of pure power as the ball cracks off the bat...it was back.

In a double-header at home against the San Antonio Missions, I hit four home runs, each one louder and further than the other.

Wally said this stuff wasn't magical thinking, but it sure felt like magic to me.

I used this amazing hot streak to work on how I was responding to positive events. I had to argue with my negative thoughts even as I was crushing the ball.

Why *do* we all have a tendency to tell ourselves that success is the exception and failure is the norm?

The more I evaluated my thinking, the more I realized how my immediate reaction to events — positive *or* negative — was pessimistic.

But, I was making progress.

I got quicker at recognizing a negative thought, arguing with it, and replacing it.

After I hit a home run, my initial reaction was usually something like, *that's probably the only weak pitch I'll see all day.*

Now, I recognized the pessimism in that thought and immediately argued with it: *Wrong, your experience, hard work, and God-given power is paying off. YOU did that, not the pitcher. It wasn't the pitch, it was the hit.*

And then I'd replace the pessimistic thought with an optimistic one: *I'm on fire! If I keep swinging the bat like this, I could have another dinger or two by the end of this night. It doesn't matter what they throw at me next, I have the power to launch it into the bleachers again.*

This type of positive thinking was a lot harder to embrace than one might expect. The old me would've argued with the optimistic thoughts by saying something like, *Don't get ahead of yourself, you've been down this road before and you know how it ends. All good things come to an end. Don't get your hopes up, old man.*

I had been conditioned to think like this over the past few years and, thanks to Wally's teachings, I was now doing my best to put a stop to the pessimism once and for all.

One evening in early June, I made a point to call Janey when I knew she'd have a chance to talk. I asked about her and the kids, told her the good news about my hot streak, and then did something I should have done a long time ago. I told her I was sorry for what I'd been putting her through.

"It's not your fault," she said. "You've had some bad breaks."

"No, it *is* my fault," I said. "And I'm not talking about my performance on the baseball field. I'm talking about my attitude off the field. I'm talking about how negative I've been around you. I'm talking about how poorly I've responded to the adversity I've run into. That's not how a man should be responding to setbacks and I'm sorry."

I heard silence on the other end of the line.

"My manager, a guy named Wally Hogan, he's making me see things in a new way," I said. "He's made me realize what a pessimist I had become. I look back on the way I've behaved, on the way I've been talking to you and the kids. I can't imagine trying to live with someone like that. I know I've been putting you through hell. I'm truly sorry. And I'm changing things.

"Thank you for not quitting on me."

I waited for a response, but heard none.

"Janey?" I asked. "Did I lose you?"

I realized then that she was crying. It was like the tension that had been building up over the past few seasons was being released.

"I don't know...what to...what to say," she said between sobs.

"You don't have to say anything," I said. "Except that you'll try to forgive me."

"I do forgive you," she said. "I've missed you — the *real* you — for so long. I love you."

It was the first time she had said she loved me in more than a year and it was the greatest thing I'd ever heard.

"I just hope..."

"What?" I asked. "You hope what?"

"I just hope this isn't the hot streak talking."

"It's not, it's more than that" I said. "I'm making permanent changes in my life."

"Thank you," Janey said. "Thank you so much."

My life was turning around. Everything was going my way. Wally's techniques were working better and faster than even he could have expected. *Nothing* was going to knock me off track now.

Or, so I thought…

15

As the temperature heated up, so did our team. We found ourselves in a back-and-forth battle for first place in the North Division of the Texas League.

Minor league baseball is a unique environment for athletes. As a competitor, you want to win every time you take the field. You and your teammates know that you have to work together in order to win. You want to win a championship, to be the best. And the community you play for wants you to win a championship, which gives you added energy as the season goes on.

Yet, at the same time, in the minors you're also competing with each other, your teammates. Everyone knows this. Everyone is trying to move up and if one of your teammates gets called up, he's taking a spot that could've been yours.

In the majors, guys have long-term contracts and you have some clubhouse stability. Every team has a few franchise guys who are there for years and serve as the foundation for the organization. Teammates form tight bonds as they chase pennants together.

In the minors, it's a bit more complicated.

A minor league clubhouse is a revolving door. You've got guys being sent up and sent down constantly. During some stretches, you'll see new faces joining and leaving the team every other week, sometimes every other day. Turnover is so excessive that a Double-A league like ours, the Texas League, awards a playoff spot to the team with the best record in the division at the midpoint of the season. Then, they reset everybody's record for the second half of the season to determine each division's second playoff spot.

Don't misunderstand me; in the minors, you still form some tight friendships along the way. There are a few guys I've become lifelong friends with during my career and I was genuinely, over-the-top excited for them when they got called up. But, the reality is that every call-up that isn't you is a missed opportunity. It means the organization chose them over you and there might not be another opportunity any time soon.

And that eats at you—no matter how happy you are for the guy who *did* get the call-up.

Due to the cut-throat nature of the business, I've seen more than a few teammates become bitter rivals over the years. I've had a few such rivalries myself.

Jealousy is usually the cause of these feuds. It's a long season in close quarters with a couple dozen guys who are ruthlessly competing with each other to make their dreams come true. Tension is bound to boil over every so often. And that's what happened on this hot June night at a sports bar in Springdale, Arkansas.

From April to Labor Day each year, minor league teams play 144 regular season games. During that span, we get just eight days off. If you count spring training and a playoff run into mid-September, you're talking about maybe ten total days off in a seven-month season. These off days are precious.

You might expect that on these off days everybody would want to take off in different directions and get as far away as they can from baseball and each other to recharge their batteries. Yet, we usually all end up *together* watching *baseball* at a local pub.

That's exactly where we ended up on this night.

As it usually happens with episodes like this, it starts with somebody drinking too much to blow off some steam…and then blowing that steam your way.

That somebody was a guy named Mitch Mercer. A big, heavy-set 24-year-old, Mitch had Babe Ruth's physique, but had yet to find the Bambino's swing. He was one of those lucky minor-leaguers who signed a million-dollar contract when he was drafted out of high school. However, word around the clubhouse was that the organization was getting impatient about their investment as they waited and waited for Mitch to learn how to hit a curve ball.

"Do any of you boys believe a word Wally says?" I heard Mitch slur, noting that his Southern drawl became more pronounced the more he drank. I don't remember how the conversation took this turn. To my knowledge, nobody had been saying anything about Wally or his philosophy.

Mitch was sharing a table with me and four other teammates. He bought the table a few pitchers of beer — throwing around his cash as some millionaire minor-leaguers like to do — and he was out-drinking everyone at least three-to-one.

I couldn't help but wonder how much Mitch still had left in the bank. He was signed as an 18-year-old for something like $2 million and here he was still playing Double-A ball seven years later. Not that I had any room to talk, being a 31-year-old in Double-A, but Mitch didn't strike me as someone who was particularly smart with his money. I wanted to tell him to be careful with it, to put it away and invest it, but Mitch was the kind of guy who wouldn't listen to such advice. He knew everything and didn't need anyone to tell him different.

Nobody responded to Mitch's out-of-the-blue statement about Wally and he squinted at us with a look of disbelief.

"You gotta be kidding me," he said. "You guys are buying into his hocus-pocus mindset stuff, ain't you?"

"I don't know about the rest of the guys, but I'm in," Ricky Alvarez said. "I'm seeing baseball and life in a totally different way and I'm pitching better than ever before. I don't think it's a coincidence."

"Puh-lease," Mitch said, drawing the word *please* out long and dramatically. "That's exactly what it is: a co-in-ci-dence." I couldn't tell if Mitch was stumbling over sounding out his words due to his drunkenness or if he was trying to put added stress on the syllables for some unknown reason. It was probably a little bit of both.

"You're pitching lights out because you're due,

son," Mitch continued. "You're hitting your stride because you got talent and the time is right. Lots of pitchers hit their stride at your age. It ain't got nothing to do with what our crackpot manager's been yapping about.

"He tried it all on me, but I ain't falling for it. Sat me down, invited me to ride in his big ol' RV, and told me how I needed to adjust my attitude if I wanted to make it big. Give me a break."

Mitch waved his hand in the air like he was swatting away a foul smell. "I've heard it all before. That stuff don't work. I already got everything I need right here inside me." He pounded his chest. "It's all in my heart. You can't teach what I got.

"Listen hard, young bucks. Take it from someone who's been around and knows the truth. The only thing that works is heart and discipline."

And with that line, Mitch chugged three quarters of a beer and unsteadily poured himself a fresh one from the pitcher on the table. The contradiction of his words and actions at that moment wasn't lost on any of us.

"Why do you think Wally would spend so much time talking about it if he hadn't seen it produce results?" Ricky asked.

"Because he's got to say somethin'," Mitch said. "He can't play ball no more and this game ain't all that complicated. So, he's got to do something to justify his existence." Mitch had trouble with the word *existence*, sounding more like *es-sistence*. "He's just trying to make himself sound like some baseball Buddha, some guru whose worth the salary he gets to drive around and watch us play ball all summer.

"I'm sure Kane agrees with me, don't ya?" Mitch said, turning to me. "You've been around the block a time or two. You know this stuff is B.S. just like I do, right? Tell these young pups. Don't fill their heads with false promises."

"Actually, I think there's something to it." I said. "I admit, I was skeptical at first, but the results speak for themselves. Look at how Ricky's pitching right now. And since I've been listening to Wally, I've been hitting the ball like never before. I think there's something to it."

Mitch made a big show of rolling his eyes and forcing a laugh. "He's got you drinking the Kool-Aid too, huh old timer? That's just sad. Take it from me, pops, Ricky is hitting his natural stride and you're on a freak of a hot streak that will end at any moment. You'll see."

"If you've got all the answers, tell me, when do you plan on hitting *your* stride?" I asked.

He looked at me sharply, like a sleepy bear that had just been poked awake. "What'd you say to me, pops?"

"You heard me just fine," I said, not backing down.

"I'm trying to talk some sense into these boys before they get their hopes up and fool themselves about what it takes to make it," he said. "And you're one to talk about hitting your stride. What're you, fifty now?"

"What do you call the way he's been hitting the cover off the ball the last three weeks?" Ricky asked in my defense. "Looks like a man finding his stride to me."

"Puh-lease," Mitch slurred again. "Are you even listening to me? There's a difference between hitting your stride and catching a lucky streak. Trust me, boys, I've been around long enough to tell the difference. Kane here is on one of the luckiest streaks I've ever seen. Nothing more. He knows it just as much as I do. He'll be back to batting .100 within the month.

"Why do you think he got sent here in the first place?" Mitch continued to preach to the table. "Because he can't hit no more. Kansas City knows it, we all know it. They sent him down here to squeeze out what's left of his contract with a little experiment. He's here to be a Crash Davis for all of us. Ain't that right, Kane? You're supposed to be a mentor for us. But you ain't my mentor and you ain't nobody else's mentor. You're just like Wally, feeding everybody false hope. You're a joke is what you are."

As someone who still hadn't learned to suppress my Irish temper, I said to Mitch, "You're calling me a joke? You? The guy who signed a two-million-dollar contract and still hasn't sniffed a day in the majors? You're the very definition of *wasted potential*."

"At least I got a two-million-dollar contract," Mitch snapped at me, the tension rising. "If I hadn't hurt my knee last season, I would have already signed another one."

"Is that right?" I asked. "Your knee's the problem, huh? You don't think the forty pounds you've packed on, the twelve-pack of Budweiser you're drinking every night, or your complete *lack* of discipline has anything to do with you wasting your potential?"

Mitch responded by launching his half-full mug of beer at my face. I moved my head just fast enough to let the mug smash into the wall somewhere behind me. I lunged at him. An instant later we had flipped over the table and were wrestling awkwardly on the barroom floor. It was an ugly event that I wish I could say was a first-and-only experience for me.

Our teammates quickly separated us before any bones were broken and we all decided it was best to call it a night.

Everyone except Mitch, that is, who declared he wasn't going anywhere. I later heard he had passed out at the bar within fifteen minutes of our skirmish.

Back at my apartment, I reflected on why Mitch Mercer had gotten under my skin so easily. Why did I care what he thought of Wally or my play on the field? Why did I feel the need to argue with some drunk guy complaining about his manager or ribbing me about my age?

The more I thought about it, the more I realized the truth: I was scared that Mitch was right.

I was scared that maybe I *was* on a hot streak that had nothing to do with the new way of thinking Wally was teaching me.

And if what I was on at the moment was nothing more than a lucky streak, that meant it would be ending soon, just like a drunken, overweight, underperforming ballplayer had told me it would.

And *that* scared me to death.

16

I woke up the next morning with extreme soreness in my left elbow and had trouble lifting it. I looked in the mirror and saw that it had turned black and blue. During my tussle with Mitch, I must have banged it hard on the ground.

Great, this is all I need, I thought to myself while examining the damage. *You've finally got your swing back and you ruin it in a wrestling match with Mitch Mercer. Smart, Bobby, real smart. Are you ever going to learn how to stop being such a disaster?*

The negative thoughts rolled in and I made no attempt to argue with them. *I deserve this. I don't deserve to be successful.*

Minor-leaguers generally don't talk about their injuries unless they physically can't take the field. You don't want word to trickle through the organization that you have a nagging injury and therefore are too risky to be called up. But I couldn't hide my gruesome elbow.

As we all boarded the team bus for our next road

trip, Wally came up to me in the parking lot and lifted my elbow for a closer look. I winced at the pain.

He shook his head and said, "I'm not even gonna say it."

He didn't have to. His look said it all.

Wally walked back to his office on wheels to coach someone else. He knew what had happened and he was disappointed in me, the way a father is when his son makes a stupid decision.

During our four-game series in Midland, Texas, Mitch's prediction that I would fall back to batting .100 was pretty close to accurate. I played through the elbow pain, but my swing had been slowed by it. The pain was gone by our fourth game, but my hot bat hadn't returned. I also found that the twisting and turning in my stomach was back.

I was so mad at myself. I spent the night after each game stewing in my hotel room. I mentally beat myself up.

You blew it, Bobby. You had your chance and you blew it…AGAIN. Welcome back to reality. And you wonder why you're still stuck in the minors after all these years.

Janey called twice during this stretch, but I didn't answer. The last thing I wanted to do was confess to her that I'd sabotaged myself once again by getting into a ridiculous barroom brawl.

For the first time since Wally convinced me to work on my thinking, for the first time since I told Wally I was committed to making optimism a habit, for the first time since I told Janey I was making permanent changes to my attitude; here I was facing my first test dealing with adversity.

And I was failing miserably.

I had snapped right back into my old pessimistic way of thinking.

I was looking at this setback as a permanent failure: *I had missed my chance, like I ALWAYS do.*

I was allowing the failure to spread to other areas of my life: *I had let down Janey again; she's going to be so disappointed with me.*

And, I was making it internal: *the problem isn't one bad decision, the problem is YOU – you're the one always making these bad decisions. YOU don't deserve success.*

So much for changing my thinking. So much for being mentally strong. So much for working my way back to the majors.

How easy it is to slip back into negative thinking.

17

Interestingly, Ricky Alvarez, who had been pitching lights out this season, also had a disastrous series against the Midland RockHounds. In our first game, he gave up six runs in an inning-and-a-half before Wally pulled him out of the game.

Ricky pitched again three nights later and this time gave up nine runs (three of those runs occurring on walks with the bases loaded) in three innings.

To add insult to injury, while Ricky and I both had horrible outings in Midland, Mitch Mercer caught fire during this stretch and hit three home runs over the four-game series. Mitch enjoyed throwing *I-told-you-so* grins at us as he rounded the bases.

As we were getting ready for our next road trip, this one to Corpus Christi, Texas, Wally tapped me and Ricky both to join him for some much-needed coaching on his RV.

"I don't know exactly what happened to you two that night at the bar and I don't really want to know," Wally said as soon as we hit the road. "Because it doesn't really matter. **You can't go back in time and change anything. All you can do is handle how you *react* to an event—both good and bad events.** And based on what I saw over the last four days, you two are both doing a very poor job of reacting positively to this event."

"It's that Mitch Mercer dude," Ricky said. "He got in my helmet. Started filling my head with doubt and negative thoughts. He's making me question all the stuff you've been saying."

"Nobody's *making* you do anything," Wally said. "You have control over how you react to other people's comments. Nobody else does.

"How about you, Bobby? Are you letting big, bad Mitch Mercer get in your head too?" Wally's tone was purposely condescending, trying to call me out for letting a guy like that have such a negative impact on me. And rightly so.

"I hate to admit it, but yeah," I said. "That, and the elbow. I'm mad at myself for doing what I did."

"I don't have to tell you guys what you're doing wrong," Wally said. "You already know you're letting lies—L.I.E. lies—control you right now. If you're still writing in your journals each night, which I hope you are, I'm guessing you've both recognized that your self-talk has taken a sharp negative turn these last few days. Am I right?"

Ricky looked back at me from the front passenger seat. I was sitting right behind him. We both nodded.

"Sounds about right," Ricky said.

"Good, then I'm not going to go through the steps for arguing with that self-talk again." Wally kept his eyes on the road and tossed a handful of sunflower seeds into his mouth. He wasn't impatient with us. He was matter-of-fact and seemed prepared to address exactly what we were doing.

"You know how to destroy those lies, we've already been through that," Wally said. "Now it's up to you to practice what we talked about. I can't do it for you."

"Of course not," Ricky said. "It's on us, skipper."

"I called you two into my office today to talk about all the negativity that surrounds us and go through the ways we can protect our minds from it.

"Look, I know Mitch Mercer thinks I'm full of it. He's not the only one. I've been preaching this gospel for years and I meet guys like him all the time. Do I take what they say personally? No way. Do I question *my own* beliefs because of what they think of them? Not a chance in hell.

"This world is full of pessimism. You know that already. That's what fills your mind with cynicism and negativity in the first place. If it's not somebody you work with, it's something you see on TV or something you hear on the radio. You don't have to go searching for bad news and pessimism; it finds you.

"That's why you have to build up a mind moat."

"A *mind moat*?" I asked in a somewhat mocking tone. "What is that?"

"It's exactly what it sounds like," Wally said. "**A mind moat is a mental barrier, a wall that protects your positive mindset from outside negative forces. You have to have a strong one if you're going to maintain an optimistic attitude in this world.**"

"Okay," I said. "And how does one go about building one?"

"I thought you'd never ask," Wally said with a big grin. "Grab your notebooks."

18

"Developing a mind moat means *consciously* managing your environment," Wally said. "There are two important aspects of this.

"**First, you have to eliminate all the negativity you can from your personal environment. This means recognizing the people and things that feed you negativity and getting rid of them**.

"**Secondly, you have to properly manage the negative things in your environment that you *can't* get rid of — things like negative people you're stuck working with.**"

Mitch Mercer's know-it-all smirk immediately came to mind as Wally mentioned *negative people*.

"What you feed your body with determines your physical well-being," Wally said. "The food you let into your body, the workouts you put yourself through; it all determines your physical potential. The same is true for your mental well-being. **The thoughts you let into your mind and the way you talk to yourself determines your mental potential. And like**

Bobby Knight used to say, the mental is four times more important than the physical.

"The things you allow into your mind will have a huge impact on your attitude. If you let in mostly negative thoughts, you're going to adopt a negative attitude. You should make every effort to keep needless negative thoughts from entering into your mind.

"It's actually a lot simpler to do this than you might realize," Wally continued. "Most people mindlessly consume a steady dose of bad news and cynical statements all day long. It starts first thing in the morning. You grab the newspaper and what's on the front page?"

Ricky glanced at me with a smile and said, "Uh, Wally, most of us don't read newspapers anymore."

"Okay, then you turn on the TV to check the news or you check the news sites on your phone, what do you see first?"

"I may be showing my age here, but I *do* read the newspaper," I said.

"And?" Wally asked.

"If it bleeds it leads," I said.

"Exactly," Wally said as he grabbed another

handful of sunflower seeds. "Some sad and tragic story is usually the first thing you see. It's almost always bad news. The media bombards us with this bad news because they know we're all strangely attracted to it. Like a car wreck, you can't look away from it.

"But think of what all this negative news is doing to your mind. You see all those tragic headlines and you can't help but be cynical. You can't help but be worried and fearful. Seeing news like that instantly raises the stress level in your body. What a horrible way to start your day."

"What are you suggesting?" I asked. "That we ignore what's going on in the world? I don't want to be naïve, walking around with my head in the clouds, oblivious to reality."

"That right there is the problem," Wally said. "What you're seeing *isn't* an accurate portrayal of reality. Those horrific stories that make the headlines are rare. *Extremely* rare. The newspapers and news sites know these rare events get your attention, so they hit you with those headlines again and again. The bloodier and more heartbreaking, the more attention it gets. They make you think these rare events are the norm. But they're not!

"Look around your own life, the people you know, the places you've been. Sure, there are some tragic events you can recall, and some people have experienced worse than others. Yet, the good far outweighs the bad. **There's always more to be grateful for than fearful of. Anyone can see this unless they've filled their mind with a cynical worldview.**

"Some of the most successful people I've ever met — world-class CEOs, top coaches, great entrepreneurs — they start their day by purposely avoiding all the negativity in newspapers, on TV, or on the radio because they know it will infect their mindset with negativity and throw their whole day off.

"When they grab a newspaper, they go straight to the business or sports pages. Why? Because they know that's where they'll see stories about achievers, stories about ambitious people who make things happen, stories about people overcoming the odds, stories about goal-driven people, stories about people battling through adversity. They avoid the negative click-bait headlines that everyone else flocks to and they protect their mindset.

"I started doing this myself back in my 20s. When I limited the negative news, you know what happened? I had a much happier start to my day. I was much more energetic. I was more pleasant to be around. I was more encouraging to others…and to myself. I developed a more optimistic view of the world. I started believing in myself more. All because I was feeding myself positive stories and ignoring all the tragic stories.

"I continue this practice today and it protects my mindset from needless negativity. It's all part of developing a mind moat to consciously decide what I'm going to let in and what I won't."

"But skipper, how are we supposed to stay informed?" Ricky asked. "Like you said, the TV, the Internet; it all screams negative news at you. Where do we go instead if we want to make sure we're keeping up with the world around us?"

"I'm not saying you should bury your head in the sand and ignore reality," Wally said. "We all know that this world has plenty of adversity it will continue to throw your way. What I'm saying is that you shouldn't *dwell* on all the negative stuff. Don't inundate yourself with it. It will only make things worse. Notice your surroundings, be aware of just how negative it is, and then remind yourself the news you come across is *not* an accurate portrayal of reality. It promotes the *rare* tragic events and tries to make them seem normal.

"Trust me, the important world events you need to know about will find you. There's no reason to wade through read every sad and negative headline to find the news that really matters.

"This same principle must be applied to your entertainment as well. What books are you reading and what movies are you watching? Do they make you feel courageous and inspired or do they leave you feeling fearful and worried? What kind of music do you listen to? Is it hopeful and encouraging or is it sad and cynical?

"I was lucky because I first started working on my mind moat back in the 1980s. The music, the shows, and the movies at that time were mostly over-the-top optimistic. It was part of the culture then. Pop culture these days can be a lot more pessimistic. You have to be more careful about what you let into your mind. Just like anything else worthwhile, it requires discipline."

"You mentioned sports as a place for positive news," I said. "But there are scandals and negative headlines in the sports section too. For every winner, there is a loser. Isn't that negative also?"

"Absolutely not," Wally said. "Sports are good for the soul. The negative headlines are the *exception* in sports and not the norm. And, yes, there are losers in every game, but sports celebrate the comeback just as much as the victory — maybe even more so. Watch *SportsCenter* each morning and what do you see in all the highlights? Guys giving it their all. People charging after their goals. Winners enjoying the moment and losers shaking off defeat to try again. Sports teach us courage, passion, fearlessness, hard work, determination, character, grit. The list could go on and on. No, sir, sports are great for your mind!"

Wally made a compelling argument.

"**So much of this mind moat stuff is about being aware of your environment**," Wally said. "**Once you're aware of whether something is feeding you positive or negative thoughts, that's half the battle. Then, you can eliminate the negative and surround yourself with the positive.**

"And I assume that includes people," I said.

"Absolutely!" Wally said. "You have to apply the same technique to the people you hang around with.

"Are there people close in your life that always talk about negative things or put others down? How do your closest friends talk about the future? Are they optimistic or pessimistic? Are they excited about life or convinced that the future is bleak? Are they happy for you when good things happen or are they jealous of you? Do they truly care about you or are they too wrapped up in themselves? Are they ambitious people with big goals or are they do-the-bare-minimum people?

"Once you identify the positive and negative influencers in your life, then you can limit your time with the negative people and spend more time with the positive people.

"You don't have to have a big talk with any of the negative people and tell them you're no longer friends. It doesn't need to be anything dramatic like that. Just make a conscious decision to limit your time with them. Turn down their invitations to hang out more often. Walk away when conversations with them start going down those negative paths.

"When you do these things, when you limit the negativity in your environment, you'll find that it's a lot easier to maintain an optimistic attitude."

19

"But what about all the negative stuff you can't turn the page on?" Ricky asked. "When a guy you go to work with everyday feeds you nothing but negativity, you can't just change the channel or turn to the sports section. These people are part of your daily life. You're stuck with them."

"That's the second, and more challenging part, of building your mind moat," Wally said. "It requires that you constantly remind yourself to *consider the source*.

"**Whenever you find yourself around someone who is always complaining or gossiping or putting you down: _consider the source_.**

"Ask yourself, 'Who the hell is this guy and why should I listen to him?'"

I liked how Wally had a way of cutting to the core of his philosophy in everyday ballplayer talk. He didn't preach to us in professorly terms. He was blunt. He talked like a normal person who had no doubt that what he was saying was the truth. It made his message more effective to me than if I were to hear it from a perfectly-polished, highly-paid self-help guru.

I don't know how else to describe it other than to say that Wally's conviction was contagious. When he talked about this stuff so assuredly, it made me want to have the same beliefs he did.

"**Consistently negative people are almost always unsuccessful, unhappy, unpleasant, uncaring, and underachieving people**," Wally said. He pointed at us, once again indicating that we were to write down his message. Ricky and I complied.

"Should you care what these types of people think of you?" Wally asked. "Should you care what people like *that* think will happen to you, your team, or your company? Should you care what those people think you should do with your life?"

"No," I said. "But sadly, it's human nature to care. We might not like to admit it, but we all care what other people think of us."

"You're right, most of us *have* been programed to worry about what everybody else thinks," Wally said. "We learn this from a young age because we want to fit in so badly. But, just like negativity in general, you can reprogram yourself out of that misguided thinking. The earlier you learn how to do that, the better off you'll be.

"This is where positive self-talk serves you once again. You have to consciously remind yourself to only care about the opinions of people you *should* care about."

"How do I determine which opinions I should care about and which I shouldn't?" I asked. "After all, sometimes I might not want to hear what someone thinks, but I *need* to hear it. Like the constructive criticism from a boss or a teacher."

"Or a manager," Ricky said with a smile.

"Once again, you consider the source," Wally said. **"The only people you should listen to when it comes to opinions and advice are people who you admire**. Notice that I didn't say people you *like*, I said people you *admire*. You admire someone for their accomplishments, for their integrity, for their work ethic, or because they truly care about you. When I was growing up, my high school football coach was one of those hard-nosed, short-tempered, old-school coaches and I can't say I liked him. But, I did admire him for his toughness, for what he achieved, for how much he wanted us to be successful, for the time and commitment he put into our team, and for how much he cared about us being winners. I mean, the guy really cared about us — I'm sure of that."

I pictured a coach like Vince Lombardi when Wally said this. He was known for pushing his players hard and I can't imagine he was ever easy to play for. But his players undoubtedly admired him.

"You might not *like* everything about every coach, teacher, or boss you have, but you probably admire something about them if they're doing the job they should be doing.

"Now, just because you admire someone doesn't mean they have all the answers. They can be — and sometimes *will* be — wrong about things. But, by immediately eliminating the voices of those you don't admire, you've mentally blocked out an enormous amount of potential negativity.

"You see, your mind needs a clear reason for either blocking something out or allowing it in for further consideration. Otherwise, it will let *everything* in. When you allow a bunch of negativity and pessimism in, you spend too much time deliberating or worrying about whether you should accept it — whether those voices are right.

"You have to catch yourself when someone is giving you advice or stating their opinion—especially when it's negative. **You have to immediately ask yourself, 'Do I admire this person?' If the answer is no, then you mentally block their negativity out.** You let anything they spew go in one ear and right out the other. Your mind won't let it in because you've already sent the command: *block this message*.

"This doesn't mean you have to be a jerk to anyone you don't admire. It doesn't mean you have a right to be disrespectful to someone who may not be personally invested in your wellbeing—they might not even know you very well. What I'm saying is that you should disregard the negative things they say about you and any pessimistic advice they try to give you. If they tell you that you don't have what it takes, that you'll never be good enough, that you should quit; block them out immediately."

"That's it?" I asked.

"That's it," Wally said. "It really is that simple. Once you give your mind a reason to block something out, it will do so and it will do so quickly. Just ask yourself, 'Do I admire this person?' Answer that and your mind will instantly know whether to allow in or block out what they're saying.

"This technique empowers you. It takes the power away from negative influences and brings the power back to you. If the voice is from someone you don't admire, then whatever negative things they're saying go directly into the mental trash dump.

"It's like instantly raising the drawbridge on your mind moat. You may still hear them yelling at you from across the moat, but what they say won't get in. You have flipped a mental switch that will keep the negativity out."

"And what happens if almost all the people in your life are people you don't admire or people who don't care about you?" Ricky asked.

I couldn't tell if he was joking or not, but Wally didn't take any chances.

"Find a new group of people to be around...fast." Wally said. **"You become like the people you hang around most. Always. It's only a matter of time. Make sure you're spending most your time with people you admire."**

20

Wally walked up behind me during batting practice before our first game against the Corpus Christi Hooks. I was searching for *that sound* again, but hadn't found it.

"Swing looks good, remember to keep that head down," Wally said. "And remember to breathe. Don't play too tight."

I acknowledged his pointers with a nod as I let out a deep breath and readjusted my stance between pitches.

"And remember also that a streak is all in your head," Wally said.

I looked back at Wally. It was like he could see into my mind. He knew what I was thinking. He knew that I was afraid my hitting slump would continue. He knew I was worried that the scorching-hot bat I had just a week ago might not be coming back. He knew I was wondering if Mitch Mercer was right.

"Consider the source, Bobby," he said. "If someone tells you a hot streak is ending or a cold streak is coming, consider the source. Even if that source is you. Don't let others sabotage you and don't let that negative voice in your head sabotage you, either.

"**You are in control of your thoughts and you become what you believe.** Whether you're hot or cold is up to you. Want to get on a hot streak? *Decide* to get on one. Tell yourself you're on one and make it so."

And with that Wally walked away. The only thing missing was a mic drop. He knew he had just smashed a line-drive of wisdom right into my head. It was a wakeup call.

No long conversation on a six-hour road trip. Just the truth, right when I needed to hear it.

He's right, I AM on a hot streak, I thought to myself. *I AM going to have the best season of my career. I WILL make it happen. Nobody is going to rob me of that.*

The pitch came in and I swung away.

That sound was back.

21

In our three-game series against Corpus Christi, I got back into a solid hitting groove. I didn't hit any home runs, but I had six RBIs, two doubles, and a triple.

I continued to work on my self-talk during this stretch. I used every strikeout, pop-up, and ground-out as an *opportunity* to manage the way I talked to myself. I applied the L.I.E. technique Wally had taught me and I kept reminding myself that *I* was the one in control of my thoughts, no one else was.

Our team swept the series against Corpus Christi, which put us within half-a-game of first place in the Texas League's North Division. This was important because we were now into the month of June and whichever team had the best record in the division at the end of the month (the halfway point of the regular season) would automatically earn a playoff spot. Also at the end of June was the Texas League All-Star Game and making the North Division's roster would certainly help my chances of getting called back up to Omaha in July.

This was the point in the season where tension started to build about potential call-ups. Everyone was into a good groove of playing baseball at this point and guys knew if they were going to catch the organization's attention, they needed to do it before trades ratcheted up in July.

Wally coached a few other guys during the road trip back to Springdale and I used the trip back home to reconnect with Janey. She called me out — rightly so — for avoiding her calls during my disastrous series against Midland.

"I'm sorry about that, you know how it is, I had a lot on my mind," I said. But she didn't let me off the hook so easily.

"And so did I," she said. "When you didn't call me back, I checked your stats and thought, 'Here we go again. He's down and doesn't want to talk.' You told me things were going to be different."

After a brief pause, I realized I was in the wrong and conceded.

"You're absolutely right," I said. "As my manager let me know, I was doing a poor job of walking the walk on this positive mindset stuff. I was letting outside events get into my head. It's easier said than done, but just give me a chance. I really am making some changes. It's not easy, but I'm doing it. I promise you."

We then had a long talk about the kids, her parents, and things back home. It was nice talking about things outside of baseball, but we couldn't completely avoid the giant elephant in the room.

"So…what are you hearing?" Janey finally asked. "Any news on call-ups?"

"My batting average is improving," I said. "That 10-game stretch I had a couple weeks ago got my home runs back on track. But I haven't heard anything more than rumors."

"What kind of rumors?"

"That the Royals are making pitchers the priority right now."

"That can change," Janey said, trying to be hopeful. But I could hear the disappointment in her voice.

"Definitely," I said. "You know how it goes. All it takes is one injury or one bad slump for an opportunity to open up."

It was always odd to admit that one guy's bad break could be your golden opportunity — such a dire way to think about things. But that was the nature of minor league baseball. An injury at the top would trickle down to moves for all the minor league teams. None of us root for someone to get injured, but when news of injuries hit, everyone in the clubhouse takes notice and hopes they might be one step closer to making their dream a reality.

22

After the road trip back to Springdale, we had another off day. I went in for a morning workout and Wally was there to greet me.

"Do you play golf?" Wally asked me.

"I enjoy *trying* to play golf," I said.

Wally gave me a quick courtesy chuckle and said, "How about instead of another fight night at the local pub, you join me for a round of golf today?"

"Sounds great." How could I refuse?

Wally picked me up that afternoon in a Cadillac Escalade and took me to a high-end exclusive country club. This raised some new questions, which I didn't waste time asking on the first tee.

"Wally, I don't mean to pry into your personal life, but either you're the world's highest paid Double-A manager or you made a lot more as a player than I realized. Care to tell me which it is?"

Wally grinned with one cheek full of sunflower seeds.

"I never made much more than the league

minimum as a player. And back then, it wasn't anything close to the half-million a year it is now. I managed to stay employed for a good eight-and-a-half years in the majors, but I was always that guy fighting to keep one of the last roster spots.

"As for my manager's salary; it's barely enough to cover the gas I'm spending driving my RV from game to game."

"So...?" I asked.

"So, I was smart with my money. A bunch of us players took a trip to Vegas one time as soon as the season ended. We had a blast and I had a hunch that place was going to grow fast. I called around and bought up some land not far off the Strip. A little here, a little there. Today, that land *is* part of the Strip. I also bought some rental properties in Southern California back when I played with the Dodgers. In the '90s, I caught some hot dot-com stocks and got out before they crashed. You know, just played it smart and let my money do the work so I could stay a part of baseball."

He said it so matter-of-factly, as though *anybody* could do what he did.

"A lot of guys try to do the same thing with their

money, but they guess wrong," I said.

"Yep, and I guessed wrong plenty of times too. But I cut my losses quickly and moved on to the next opportunity. Just like a strikeout. You don't let it get worse, you don't let it affect other parts of your life, and you don't take it personally."

Wally stepped up to the tee to prepare for his first drive of the day.

"I've been a scout off-and-on through the years, spent some time as a roving instructor for the organization, but this is my first year as a manager. I don't do it for the money, believe me. I do it because I love baseball. And because I think I can make a positive difference in people's lives."

Wally raised an eyebrow at me, indicating that he thought *I* could be one of those people.

He then turned his attention to the little white ball sitting on the tee. He swung his driver awkwardly. That's being kind. It was a flat-out *ugly* swing, but he drove the ball right down the middle of the fairway.

I shook my head and laughed. "Wally, you're the luckiest guy I know."

He pointed to his head. "It all starts up here. Start thinking right and the luck will follow. That's what has worked for me."

23

I was no expert at golf, but I wasn't the poor player I'd humbly implied to be when Wally asked me if I wanted to play with him. The truth is, for a guy who doesn't spend much time on the course, I've always been a pretty decent golfer and I've been told that I have a very smooth, professional-looking golf swing. Wally, on the other hand, had a discombobulated hacker's swing. Yet, after fifteen holes, Wally had won twelve, we had tied two, and I had won one. Anyone watching the two of us swing at the ball would've been shocked to find out Wally was beating me so handedly.

I was getting a little hot about this butt-kicking, but tried to tell myself Wally's dominance was due to the fact that this was his home course. He knew all the nooks and hills of what I was finding to be a very challenging course.

"Care to share with me the secrets of this hole?" I said to Wally as we stepped into the sixteenth-hole tee box.

"Same as every other hole," he said. "Aim for where you want the ball to land."

"Sure," I said sarcastically. "That's the big secret, huh? Why didn't I think of that before?"

"Something bothering you, Bobby?" Wally asked, sensing my frustration.

"Oh, I don't know. Maybe the fact that you know this course inside and out, but you're not giving me any courtesy pointers along the way. It doesn't give me much of a chance against you."

He looked at me, surprised.

"Bobby, I joined this club two months ago and this is my first time playing the course."

"I don't believe it," I said.

"It's true. I moved here before the season and haven't had any time to get out here, until today."

"Then how do you explain the fact that you're playing all the turns and hills perfectly while I can't stay out of the rough and the hazards?"

"My round is far from perfect, but I already told you what my *secret* is," Wally said, putting air quotes around the word, *secret*. His response was curt. He didn't appreciate my whining.

"Tell me again, skipper, because you've got a golf

swing that looks like Charles Barkley's and you're whipping my butt up and down this course."

That got a half-smile out of Wally and he motioned for me to step forward and face the ball he had teed up, looking out on the hole we were about to play.

"What do you see when you look out there?" Wally asked, motioning to the short Par-3 hole in front of us.

"I'm not blind, if that's what you're implying," I said.

"I'm being serious here," Wally said. "Look out in front of you and tell me what you see. Tell me what thoughts are running through your head as you prepare for this hole."

I looked ahead thoughtfully. We were up on a hill, looking down on the hole in front of us. I started breaking it down for Wally.

"I see one tough Par-3," I said. "I see big trees and a thick rough just to the right of the green. Some of the branches are stretched out and hanging low, which could be trouble. Definitely want to avoid that. I see water to the left, which means I'd rather miss to the right and hit a tree than land in the drink. I also see a sand trap to the front-left of the green and what looks like a fairly steep hill right in front of the green. If I land short of the green, the ball is going to end up on the beach or it'll come rolling backwards who knows how far."

I looked at Wally to see if he agreed with my assessment, but he was staring out at the hole, listening.

"But I can't overshoot the green either," I continued. "There are thick weeds and trees behind it. If I end up in there, I'll never find my ball. In fact, now that I'm paying attention, there's a pretty stiff wind at our backs. I need to be careful not to swing too hard. Though, it might feel breezier here because we're elevated. I suppose ending up in the sand in front of the hole is probably better than in the weeds and trees behind it. Like most of the course, this is one tough hole. Especially with this wind. I don't know. What do you see?"

Wally kept his gaze straight ahead.

"First, let me tell you what I hear. I hear you telling me all the places you *don't* want to go. The trees to the right. The water to the left. The sand and the hill. These are all the places you want to avoid.

"Me? I look out there and I see a beautiful, soft, welcoming green with a flag pin slightly to my left.

It's a safe landing zone just waiting for my ball. *That's* where I want to land. *That's* what I'm focused on. That spot and *only* that spot.

"I close my eyes and I feel my club, my grip. I picture myself swinging easily and I see my golf ball landing right in that spot."

Wally turned to me. "Bobby, **your destination is determined by what you focus on**. You have to be very clear about where you want to go. Once you know where you want to go, you have to visualize yourself getting there and forget about all the places where you *don't* want to end up.

"I want you to focus only on where you *want* to go for these last three holes."

24

I won two of the final three holes and we tied the other one. I'm sure it wasn't a coincidence that my play improved dramatically once I listened to Wally's advice and focused on where I wanted to land, not where I didn't.

We were now in the clubhouse for some post-round steaks and drinks. We were seated next to floor-to-ceiling windows that looked out over the golf course as the sun set and an orange dusk settled over the lush green fairways.

"You know that I was talking about more than golf out there today, right?" Wally asked.

I nodded after taking a bite of one of the best rib eye steaks I've ever tasted. "The teacher never stops teaching, does he?"

"Not as long as you're here I won't. You don't belong here. You know that, don't you?"

I shrugged. "Well, the organization sent me here for a reason. It doesn't really matter what I think, does it?"

"Actually, what you think matters more than anything."

"I guess I walked into that one, didn't I?" I said with a smile.

"Bobby, what do you want right now? You saw what happened when you focused on where you wanted your golf ball to go today. Where do *you* want to go as a ballplayer?"

"Obviously, the first thing I want to do is get called back up to Omaha. No offense, I enjoy talking with you, but I need to get out of Double-A." I leaned back and took a sip of my cold pilsner.

"None taken," Wally said. "Once you get to Omaha, then what?"

"Then, I guess I want to get out of Omaha. I've been there too long and if they don't want to call me up to Kansas City, maybe I need a change of scenery, a new organization.

"Don't get me wrong, I'm grateful to have a job playing baseball. I don't want to be unemployed at the end of the season, no matter where I am."

I caught a look on Wally's face that told me he didn't like my answer.

"What?" I asked.

"You're doing it again," he said.

"Doing what? I'm answering your question honestly. What did I do wrong?"

"I just asked you where you want to go and you just told me three places you *don't* want to be: here, Omaha, and unemployed."

This was another eye-opener for me. Another moment where I suddenly realized I was doing exactly what Wally was telling me not to do. *How long have I been thinking like this — jumping straight to the negatives when considering my future?*

"Why don't you try telling me where you *want* to go?" Wally said.

"I want what every other minor-leaguer wants. I want to make it to the majors. In this organization, that means I want to be playing for the Royals."

"That's good," Wally said. "And when do you want to get there?"

"As soon as humanly possible," I said.

"Great! Let me ask you another question. And be as honest with me as you can. Where do you *expect* to go as a ballplayer?"

25

I fumbled around looking for an answer before finally saying, "I guess I hadn't really thought about it that way."

"You haven't thought about it or you don't want to tell me the truth?" Wally asked.

Wally knew what I was thinking, but I couldn't bring myself to say it out loud.

"There's a huge difference between wanting something and *expecting* something," he said. "Everybody here *wants* to make it to the majors. Not many guys truly *expect* to make it. They don't have the confidence or the focus. Many don't have the work ethic to expect it. They know deep down they haven't put in the work and preparation to deserve a call-up.

"If you want to make it back to the bigs, you have to raise your expectations. You have to be convinced that you deserve it. You have to go beyond *wanting* to get there and you have to start *expecting* to get there.

"You don't expect to make it back there, do you?"

Wally had me. I couldn't deny it.

I leaned back and let my gaze drift to the view outside — a darker blue sky now as the sun set. Wally waited for me to answer.

"I used to," I finally admitted. "But over the last few years, I guess I've lowered my expectations. I had no other choice. I had to be more realistic and recognize that this dream might not happen.

"You know the deal, Wally. If guys haven't made it by twenty-three or twenty-four, they usually *don't* make it. The organization turns their attention to the younger guys. I know how it works."

"If you don't expect to make it back to the majors, why are you still here?" Wally asked.

"Because there's always that chance. There's always that glimmer of hope that things will fall perfectly into place and the organization will have no choice but to call me up."

"A glimmer of hope just isn't enough," Wally said. "You have to *expect* it. You have to *know* in your heart that you have earned your spot on a major league roster.

"Look how your golf game changed on those final few holes today. Once you turned your focus to where you wanted the ball to land and visualized it landing there, your subconscious mind started *expecting* it to land there.

"It's an interesting fact of life: **Our thoughts and our actions create our expectations and we all tend to end up right where we expect to end up.**"

Wally had a way of putting life-changing lessons into simple, direct statements.

"**Your expectations determine what is possible,**" Wally said. "**Therefore, you have to raise your expectations about what you believe is possible.**

"**To raise your expectations for yourself, you have to get rid of all the excuses for why something *can't* be done and focus your thoughts on all the reasons why it *can* be.**

"It's just like the way you monitor your self-talk after negative events, like a strikeout. You apply the same discipline when it comes to thinking about your goals for the future.

"If you let your mind go unchecked, it'll have no trouble finding reasons for why your dream can't come true. You're too old, you missed your chance, there's too much competition, the odds of success are too long, on and on the list goes. You've got to stop those thoughts whenever they interfere with your vision for the future."

"And I suppose you do that by arguing with the negative thoughts and replacing them with positive thoughts," I said.

"You got it," Wally said. "When the naysaying lies enter your head, counter them with facts.

"You keep saying you're too old to make it back to the majors. Someone a long time ago fed you a lie that you believe to this day. It's simply *not* true!

"You're about the same age Mickey Mantle was when he hit 54 home runs, the most he ever hit in a single season. Look around the majors right now. Look at the guys who are on track to hit 40 home runs *this* season. Albert Pujols is 35. Jose Bautista is 34. Hell, David Ortiz is *39 years old*! All these guys are on track to hit 40 home runs and any one of them could lead the league in dingers. And guess what, they're *all* older than you! Drop the age excuse; it doesn't mesh with the facts."

"Those guys are the best of the best," I said.

"And your point is?"

"Isn't it obvious? I'm not in their league."

"There's no reason you can't be, Bobby. I've studied your swing. I've seen you in the weight room.

I've heard *that sound* off your bat. I'm not feeding you a line, I wouldn't do that. You've got the physical tools to be a power hitter in the majors. It's your mind that you have to convince."

A sense of warm pride built up inside of me when Wally said those words. He saw something in me. He *believed* in me.

Why didn't I believe in myself?

"You have to constantly think empowering thoughts," Wally said. "Personally, I like to have a few quotes ready for any time I hear that negative voice telling me I can't do something.

"One of my favorites is a quote I have on the wall in my office. It's a constant reminder of how I want to think. It comes from the greatest pitcher ever, Satchel Paige. He said, '**Never let the odds keep you from pursuing what you know in your heart you were meant to do.**'

"If you knew what Satchel went through in the era of segregation, what he had to endure to make his dreams come true, it adds a whole new meaning to that quote.

"My old manager, Tommy Lasorda, always repeated, '**You gotta believe**.' This was his mantra and it's another great quote to repeat to yourself, a hundred times a day if you have to. Tommy repeated it all the time. He told us he never wanted to hear us players saying, 'I can't' or, 'I won't.' He wanted us saying, 'I will, I can, I must, I believe.'

"Repeating phrases like those eliminates the negative thoughts, it sharpens your focus, and it directs your subconscious to where you *want* to go. It raises your expectations by eliminating the excuses."

"**I will, I can, I must, I believe**," I said quietly. It felt good inside as soon as I said it.

Wally smiled.

"I will, I can, I must, I believe," I said again. A little louder this time.

"I will, I can, I must, I believe," I said again, this time getting attention from the table next to us.

"You will, you can, you must," Wally said. "And *I* believe in you!"

26

"Now it's time to make a plan," Wally said.

We were back at our team's clubhouse, which was empty due to the night off. Wally saw my enthusiasm at dinner. He knew I needed to put together a plan right away.

"We have to map out a clear path for *how* you're going to make your dream happen," he said, grabbing a marker as he approached the whiteboard he often used when addressing us before games. I had my notebook, ready to record.

"Without a specific plan for making it happen, a dream is nothing more than a daydream," Wally said. **"Having a viable plan for how you're going to get from where you are to where you want to go is the quickest way to turn your wants into expectations. When you give your mind clear directions, it starts moving that way. "**

Across the top of the whiteboard he wrote, *JUNE, JULY,* and *AUGUST.*

"You've got more than half of June left, what does

Bobby Kane need to do *this month* to get himself back to the majors?"

"Get the organization's attention," I said. "I've got to do something that makes them realize they made a mistake sending me down."

"Good," Wally said. "And what would get their attention?"

I thought about it for a moment. "For starters, I'd say getting my batting average back above .300. Making the Texas League All-Star roster would also get some attention."

"That's a start," Wally said. "But several guys are going to do that. What do you need to do to *really* stand out? What will it take to ensure that your name is at the top of the list when the organization needs to call somebody up?"

"I'd probably need to lead the team in home runs. Check that—I need to lead the *league* in home runs!"

"Now we're talking. How many dingers do you think it would take to lead the league at the all-star break?" Wally asked.

"Fifteen would do it, don't you think?" I asked.

"Probably," Wally said. "But *probably* isn't good enough. Twenty would be certain to catch attention."

"I'd have to get pretty hot to hit twenty," I said. "I'd need to hit eight more before the end of the month."

"And we've got fifteen games left this month," Wally said. "That's about one home run every other game. You can do it."

The way Wally said it so matter-of-factly made me believe him. I nodded as he wrote down, _20 HRs_, on the whiteboard below _JUNE_.

"You do that and KC will start talking about you," Wally said. "I guarantee it.

"The month of July will be the month trades heat up all over baseball. You've got to continue your momentum through July. That means 10 more home runs, regardless of whether you're still here or back in Triple-A by then."

Under _JULY_, he wrote down, _10 HRs – Here or in Omaha_, and I did the same in my notebook.

"If you've got thirty by the trade deadline, you'll be getting some calls," Wally said, referring to the July 31 trade deadline every player in professional baseball knows all too well. It was a pivotal date in the season.

"That _should_ get you a call-up," Wally said. "If not, then you'll need to continue the momentum into August with ten more, wherever you are. If you've got forty home runs by Labor Day, you'll be playing on a major-league roster in September."

Under _AUGUST_, Wally wrote, _40 HRs_.

Seeing the number _40_ on the whiteboard gave me an uneasy feeling. _Forty_ home runs. Those are best-of-the-best type numbers. Did Wally really think I had the talent to be one of the best home-run hitters in all of baseball?

He moved down on the whiteboard and wrote, _SEPTEMBER_. Under that he wrote, _10 MORE HRs_ and circled it.

"Once you get to the bigs, you need to make enough noise to ensure that you _stay_ there," Wally said. "Ten more dingers should do it, especially if you're playing for a team in playoff contention like the Royals."

I added it all up and realized we were talking about fifty home runs in one season. _Fifty_! Wally noticed my shoulders sag.

"What?" he asked. "You don't think you can do it?"

"The most I've ever hit in a season was twenty-five. You want me to double that?"

"Yes," Wally said. "Twenty-five wasn't good enough, was it? We have to leave no doubt that you're the power hitter they *can't* pass up. Plus, remember, we're talking about half of these coming here in Double-A. That means smaller ballparks, more fastballs, less experienced pitchers.

"The organization needs to see extreme numbers. You have to leave no doubt that you deserve the call-up."

"Wally, I hear you, but *doubling* my home run output?"

"You've got to do it," he said. "You have some speed and that's a nice bonus, but the Royals have a lot of speed guys right now. You've shown me that you can play small ball when you need to and that's great too. But guess what? The Royals have plenty of guys who can do that. You're a smart, versatile player and the organization already knows that. You can call on those skills at any time. But to make it up to Kansas City, you're going to have to stand out and prove that you have something they really need, something they can't ignore. That something needs to be power. Home run power. The organization won't be able to pass that up, especially if they're chasing a pennant."

Wally wrote a big <u>50</u> on the whiteboard and circled it multiple times.

"That's the goal," he said as he tapped the <u>50</u>. "That's where you want to go. And remember, **if you aim high and fall short, you're still going to land higher than you've ever landed before. But it starts with a big, huge goal.** That's what you need to focus on: fifty. Get obsessed with that number. That's the number you have to *expect* to reach."

"Talk about raising my expectations," I said with an uneasy chuckle.

"You've got to do it," Wally said. "Ordinary won't get it done. You have to do something extraordinary. And I believe you can."

"Any baseball wisdom for how exactly I'm going to pull this off?" I asked.

"By focusing on this *one single goal* above everything else." Wally pointed at my notebook, telling me to write this down. "**Most people try to be good at lots of different things, but they never become great at any one thing. You'll see extraordinary results when you stop trying to be good at lots of things and start trying to be great at one thing. You'll achieve greatness when you sharpen your focus down to one, single, overriding goal.**"

"What about my batting average, my on-base-percentage, moving runners, and everything else?"

"Being exceptional at one particular thing tends to make you excel at all the other things surrounding it — especially when that one thing is so fundamental to the game. It's like the weightlifter who focuses on his squats. As his squat max goes up, it lifts his max in all the other lifts too. It's the same thing in baseball. Bobby, if you're hitting ten home runs a month, things like your batting average will be just fine, trust me.

"And remember too, Kansas City already knows you're a smart, well-rounded player. They know you can play small ball when needed. That's why they sent you down here — to teach the younger guys how to do it. But KC has plenty of guys who can get on base and move runners. They've got plenty of guys who are versatile on defense. Hell, you've *been* one of those guys for years, and I know you can continue to be one of those guys if you want to.

"But now it's time for you to do something exceptional, something that makes you stand out above and beyond everyone else. Your focus right now needs to be on power. You have a gift that many ballplayers don't have and you need to focus on it.

Your home run power—that's something special. That's something every organization *needs*."

"What are you saying?" I asked. "You want me to swing away on every pitch? Go big or go home?"

"No, of course not," Wally said. "That's not smart baseball and pitchers will quickly get the memo that you'll swing at anything. That strategy won't convert to home runs."

"Then what exactly will?" I asked.

Wally smiled big as he looked upward, reminiscing. "A wise ballplayer by the name of Leon Durham once told me, 'You can't make a living looking to hit a breaking ball. But you can make a living looking to hit a fastball.' Leon's nickname was *Bull*. He was Bull Durham long before that movie about minor league baseball ever came out. He hit 147 home runs in the majors and was a two-time All-Star.

"**Once you know exactly what you're looking for, it's a lot easier to find it**. Trust the real Bull Durham; look for a fastball."

27

I couldn't wait to step back into the batter's box with my renewed focus on one driving goal: ten home runs a month, fifty for the season. It was a big, crazy, audacious, and—most would say—*unrealistic* goal. But Wally had me convinced that it was going to take something big and crazy like this to get me back to the majors. And, more importantly, he believed I could do it. He told me I could do it and I believed him.

I spent the rest of June laying off breaking balls, swatting off less-than-ideal pitches to stay alive in the count as needed, and trying to frustrate pitchers into throwing me fastballs.

I was worried this wouldn't be an easy adjustment for me. I'd been coached for the past few years to play smaller, to move runners, to get on base. It was the Sabermetrics era of baseball and I had been told to do whatever it took to get on base.

I wondered if the organization knew Wally was convincing me to change my style, to focus on power, and I wondered if they would have approved—

especially since Wally acknowledged the whole reason I'd been sent down to Northwest Arkansas was specifically to show the younger guys how to play smaller.

I don't think Wally cared. He did things his own way. His goal was to win games and get his players called up. And he was certain that my ticket back to the majors was to become the home run king of the minors—to become a bat so powerful the majors couldn't pass up on me any longer.

This change in strategy came easier than I expected. In Double-A, young pitchers wanted to show off their heat. It wasn't too hard to get most of them throwing more fastballs after I fouled away a few breaking balls and worked the count higher than they liked.

I can't say that I instantly became a home-run machine. In fact, for the first four games after Wally and I designed our plan, I didn't hit a single shot over the wall. But, during this time I worked on staying optimistic, keeping my self-talk positive, and trusting that this was all part of the process.

I spent nights looking at my goals and visualizing them coming true. I saw myself hitting home runs in a Northwest Arkansas jersey *and* a Kansas City Royals jersey. I felt the effortless swing of hitting a fastball right on the sweet spot of the bat. I heard *that sound* that instantly told everyone in the stadium this ball wasn't landing on this side of the wall. I visualized the ball soaring over the fence. I smelled the fresh-cut, summer-evening grass and the hot dogs roasting in the ballpark as I rounded the bases. I heard the crowd roar in various major league stadiums.

I experienced all this in my mind, in the quiet of my room at night after games.

These were the visualization exercises Wally taught me.

"You have to experience it in your mind before you can expect to experience it in reality," Wally told me.

He also taught me to visualize negative events. This sounds counter-intuitive for an optimistic attitude, but Wally told me it was essential. He wanted me to experience a strikeout in my mind and then rehearse how I would react to it. He wanted me to mentally practice responding to negative events with positive self-talk.

The more I mentally prepared for dealing with negative events, the easier it was to respond

positively when they actually occurred. And the more I visualized positive outcomes—my goals coming to fruition—the more confidence I had that they were sure to come true; it was only a matter of time.

It was our series against Tulsa where I got into a good power-hitting rhythm again. In four games, I hit three home runs. I hit two more in our four-game series against the Frisco RoughRiders, which brought my total for the year to seventeen. That number made me the home run leader in the Texas League.

Our final three games before the all-star break would be against our in-state rival, the Arkansas Travelers from Little Rock. Our two teams were also tied for first place in the Northern Division of the Texas League. Whichever team won the three-game series would be assured a playoff spot, regardless of what happened in the second half of the season.

In the first game, I played well. I had three hits in five at-bats and, while playing right field on defense, I robbed a home run with a leaping catch at the wall, which would've led to three runs for the Travelers. We won the game, 5-4.

After the game, Wally informed me that I'd been

selected to play in the Texas League All-Star Game. I knew that meant a call back up to Omaha was likely to follow. However, the fact that I didn't hit any home runs in the first game of the series meant I would need to hit three in the next two games to reach my goal of twenty before the midseason point.

In our second game against Arkansas, everyone on our team struggled...including me. Maybe it was the pressure of trying so hard to reach twenty home runs, but I was impatient at the plate. I wasn't working the count and I was swinging too hard and too often at less-than-ideal pitches. I was trying to force it. I went zero-for-five at the plate and we lost the game, 9-3.

Our third game against Arkansas would settle the series and decide which one of our teams would earn a playoff spot.

Wally could sense I was tight. Before the game, he told me, "Ease up on the bat. Take it one pitch at a time. Forget about trying to reach twenty home runs today. Baseball goals, like most life goals, are intended for *long* seasons. You can't force them in a single game or series. You've done everything you need to do. If you don't get the pitches you want today, so be it. You can't force it. I want you to let go, relax, and have fun today."

It was like he'd removed a huge weight from my shoulders.

We were going up against the best pitcher in Double-A, Carlos Martinez. Word around the clubhouse was that his bags were already packed and he'd be leaving for Triple-A as soon as this game was over. The Mariners had fast-tracked this stud pitcher and wanted him ready for the majors by the end of July.

Thanks to Wally's pregame chat, I played loose and hit a shot that barely cleared the left-field wall in my first at-bat. It was my first home run off of Martinez and it brought my total for the season up to eighteen.

Martinez seemed a bit unsettled early in this game and he was struggling with control of his breaking ball. That meant he was going back to his reliable fastball, which made my job easier.

In the third inning, I faced him again and worked the count to three balls and no strikes. A lot of times in this situation, batters are told not to swing at that fourth pitch no matter what they see. You have the pitcher rattled and you want to force him to throw a strike—otherwise, he walks you and it's a free base.

But in this case, Wally gave me the okay to swing away. And swing away I did. Martinez fired a 99-mile-per-hour fastball right down the middle and I connected with it perfectly, sending it over the left-field wall once again. This time it wasn't even close; the ball cleared the fence by at least ten feet.

Martinez regained control and didn't give up a hit over the next two innings. I faced him a third time in the sixth inning. The game was tied, 3-3, with nobody on base. If there was any question about whether I had this pitcher rattled, he answered it loud and clear on his first pitch. He threw a ball high and inside that sent me reeling backward to barely avoid a shot to my ear.

Our fans booed, I heard Wally yelling something unfit to print here, and I gave Martinez a cold stare as I brushed myself off outside the batter's box. What Martinez did made perfect baseball sense. I had hit two home runs off of him already and he wanted to make me uncomfortable. Yet, when you throw the kind of heat this guy throws, it's hard not to take it personally. A pitcher with his power throwing at your head can end your career.

The next pitch came low and inside, which caused me to jump back awkwardly — legs first — and land on my elbows as I hit the ground. As I jumped to my feet, Arkansas' catcher immediately put an arm on me to keep me from charging the mound. I shrugged him off and heard the umpire give Martinez a warning: "One more and you're gone!"

Martinez didn't show any reaction. No coy smile, no apologetic glance at me, no indication that he heard the ump's warning. This guy was locked-in — a machine playing the game the way he was taught to play it.

His next pitch was a fastball down the middle. I watched it go by. Now I was the one who was rattled.

I stepped out of the batter's box, took a deep breath, and refocused with positive self-talk. I told myself, *I'll get another one just like that. I'm not rattled; HE'S the one who's rattled. He doesn't know what to do with a batter like me. He's never seen my kind of power before.*

I visualized another fastball just like the one I'd seen, and I envisioned that ball cracking off my bat and landing on the other side of the left-field wall, just like my previous two homers.

Reality didn't play out exactly like that, but it was close enough.

After working a full count and fouling off two-straight curve balls, I got the pitch I'd been waiting for and sent it sailing. Not over the left-field wall, like I had envisioned, but deep over the center-field wall instead.

Close enough. And the result was the same.

It was the first time since high school that I had hit three home runs in one game and I had done it against the hottest pitcher in all of minor league baseball.

We ended up winning the game, 7-4, and securing a playoff spot.

Like Wally had said I could, I took twenty home runs into the midseason break. I assumed it was only a matter of time before the organization would send me back up to Omaha.

But, I assumed wrong.

28

As my outlook turned more optimistic, my play on the field improved and so did my personal life—just as Wally had said it would. Now when I called Janey, I didn't hear the initial *what's wrong now?* panic in her voice. We talked less about the ups-and-downs of my baseball career and more about her, the kids, life back home, and our future. Our conversations had a more comfortable, lighter feel to them—not so much tension and uncertainty.

"Maybe we should try to make the trip to Texas for the All-Star Game," she suggested.

"Nah," I told her. "Let's save it for a trip that really matters, when I'm back in the majors."

When I'm back in the majors, I had said. It was the first time I'd spoken so assuredly about making it back to the majors in years.

This comment didn't go unnoticed. She was silent for a moment and then said, "I need to meet this Wally Hogan guy."

"Yeah? Why's that?"

"Because I want to meet the man who saved our marriage."

It may have been an odd way to respond to my offhanded comment about making it to the bigs, but I knew exactly what she meant.

Wally had told the entire team at one point, "**You don't just owe it to yourself to be an optimist; you owe it to everyone around you.**"

A pessimist sucks the energy out of the room. Nobody wants to put up with somebody who's bitter and cynical all the time. Not your friends, not your teammates, not your boss, and certainly not your spouse.

29

The Texas League All-Star Game was a lighthearted outing. I hit a home run in my second at-bat and had a double later in the game. My friend and teammate, Ricky Alvarez, pitched his two innings without giving up a run.

Everyone at the game was happy. It was a break in the season and a fun two-day celebration. We all knew that being invited to this game meant we were first on the list for the next round of call-ups that were sure to begin soon.

The month of July is a busy time of year for professional baseball teams. As the July 31 trade deadline approaches, all kinds of unforeseen moves take place throughout every organization.

Things change in an instant. You could walk into your Double-A clubhouse one afternoon and be told to pack your bags, you've been traded to another organization. That organization could be starting you off at any level—Single-A, Double-A, Triple-A, or even the majors. You just never know. And each trade sets off a chain of events. A trade at the major league level that may seem to have nothing to do with you could suddenly open up a slot for you to move higher and fill a void left behind. Each major league spot that gets filled opens up a Triple-A spot, and so on.

At the same time, these trades can mean plenty of trickle-down bad news too. It's put-up or shut-up time for organizations to decide on prospects and, a lot of times, if they can't deal a prospect they've been hoping to trade, they'll go ahead and release him for good.

It's an exciting but anxious time for players throughout every organization.

I picked up right where I left off after the All-Star break. On July 19, I hit my twenty-sixth home run of the season. This was a new single-season record for me. Sure, it was Double-A instead of Triple-A, but twenty-six dingers is twenty-six dingers and it was enough to put me way out in front as the home-run leader of the Texas League. The next closest home-run hitter was eight behind me. Of course, the home run standings in Double-A can be a bit misleading because most the guys who get hot hitting home runs early in the season are called up before their totals get too high.

I was still waiting for my call-up.

Wally had assured me that if I focused on power and made hitting home runs my number one objective, my batting average and other stats would take care of themselves. Once again, he was right. Though a power hitter usually has to accept a slightly lower batting average in the pursuit of hitting more home runs, my batting average had risen to .321, which ranked me sixth in the Texas League. My name had to be jumping out at anyone perusing Double-A batting stats.

Yet, I still hadn't received a call-up.

I asked Wally if he was hearing anything and he assured me I'd be the first to know if he did.

Nothing.

No calls from the top of the Royals organization, no feelers from other organizations, no rumors, no whispers.

Nothing but silence.

An excruciating silence.

By the July 31 trading deadline, I was still on fire at the plate. My home run total had reached thirty-one and my batting average was holding above .300.

That night in our clubhouse, Wally individually called a handful of guys into his office. One by one, he told some of those guys they had been traded and some of those guys they had been released. Two of my teammates were called up to Omaha. One of those lucky prospects was Ricky Alvarez.

He walked back to his locker with watery eyes. It was the good kind of tears. I had witnessed enough call-ups and send-downs through the years to know the difference.

Regardless of whether a player had just received good news or bad news from their manager, guys usually tried to stay to themselves when they walked back to their locker. If they were sent down or released, they were humiliated. If they were called up, they didn't want to celebrate in front of their less fortunate teammates.

I walked up behind Ricky and put my hand on his shoulder. "Congratulations, you earned it!"

He turned around and gave me a tight hug.

"Omaha?" I asked.

"Omaha," he nodded. "I'll be saving you a spot."

"You better," I said with a smile.

It was hard to hide my disappointment that I

wasn't joining Ricky for a trip back to Omaha, but I was genuinely happy for him. He was one of the good guys. A guy who did things the right way. A guy who took the time to say a kind word to everyone, regardless of whether they were the organization's highest-paid prospect or the guy cleaning up the stadium after the game.

"You'll like it there," I said. "It's a great group of guys and I think you'll find the ballparks more pitcher-friendly. You'll be in KC before you know it."

"You will too, Bobby. Don't stop believing."

"Stay in touch," I said.

"You know I will."

But I knew that unless I rejoined him as a teammate soon, we would probably never speak again. It's simply the life of a minor-leaguer.

I waited in the clubhouse another thirty minutes after Wally had given Ricky the good news, but Wally never called anyone else back to his office. There was no more news to give. I knew Wally was now frantically working to get his new roster finalized. Trade deadlines meant several current players leaving tonight and several new prospects arriving to fill their spots tomorrow.

After I had lingered as long as I could bear, I went home to my lonely apartment.

Janey had sent me a text. It was simply a question mark.

How do I respond? How do I tell her I'm still stuck in Double-A despite putting up the best numbers of my career? How do I keep a positive face when so many questions are swirling around in my head? Questions like: Have they given up on me because of my age? Were the Royals hoping to trade me, but no other teams bit? I'm leading the league in home runs with no one else even close; what more can I possibly do?

I texted Janey the most optimistic message I could muster: *Nothing...yet.* Adding the word *yet* was one of the hardest things I'd done this season.

I knew what was really going on. I knew the organization had given up on me. But I couldn't tell Janey that. I couldn't tell myself that.

30

"What's the deal, Wally?" I asked. "And shoot me straight."

The trade deadline had passed and we were now one week into August. Despite leading the Texas League in home runs with thirty-three and having a top-five batting average, I hadn't heard a peep indicating that I might be called up.

I tried to stay positive, focus on only what I could control, but I couldn't take it anymore. I needed some answers.

We were in Wally's cramped visiting manager's office after a night game in Corpus Christi. I hadn't talked with Wally much since we'd mapped out our ambitious fifty-home-run plan. The plan was working, but the call-up we expected never came. Wally wasn't avoiding me, he had two-dozen other ballplayers to mentor and he'd also brought along his wife and grandkids for a couple road trips.

"I've taken some calls about you, you've caught the club's attention," Wally said. "They're just not ready to make a move."

"This is crazy," I said. "How can I make it back to the majors if they won't even call me back up to Triple-A? They've written me off, haven't they? This is my last season with the organization, isn't it? I could hit a hundred homers down here and they still wouldn't call me up, would they?"

Wally looked me straight in the eye and said four words that seared my insides, "You might be right."

The stomach issue I had earlier in the season was suddenly back. For a second I thought I might get sick right there in Wally's office.

"I'll be honest with you, I thought you'd be back in Omaha by now," Wally said. "The way you're playing, you deserve to be. But, you know how it goes, the club's got all kinds of other things to consider and I don't pretend to know what all is going on up there.

"All I can tell you is that you've got their attention. They're asking about you. That's all I know."

"All I know is that I'm wasting every day I spend down here," I snapped.

"Wasting? You think you're *wasting* your days down here?"

I didn't respond. My eyes were fixed on the floor. I

was hot. And a bit nauseas.

"Follow me," Wally said. "We need a change of scenery."

We walked out onto Whataburger Field, the home of the Corpus Christi Hooks. Our game had ended half-an-hour ago, but the stadium lights were still on as workers cleaned up the bleachers.

I followed Wally to a patch of grass just beyond second base in shallow center field.

"Do you smell that?" Wally asked. He took in a slow deep breath and exhaled. "That ballpark smell. That night air settling on the fresh-cut grass after a hotter-than-hell summer day. The smell of hot dogs and pretzels and dirt."

Wally smiled. "On a baseball field even the *dirt* smells good," he said.

"You gonna recite me a poem?" I asked.

"Take it in, Bobby. Take in this place."

I humored my mentor and took a deep breath. I felt better, so I took another one.

"There's magic in this place," Wally said. "I don't care if it's here in Corpus Christi, Yankee Stadium, or some rusted-out sandlot in the middle of nowhere; there's magic when you step onto a baseball field. For guys like you and me, something deep within us gets ignited when we step out here. It's something in our blood. We know this is a special place. We know that when we're here, we're somewhere...*sacred*. And we know there's nowhere else we'd rather be."

I closed my eyes and took another deep breath. A memory flashed into my mind. It was the first time my dad took me to Boston's Fenway Park. A trip like that wasn't easy for my dad to pull off. He was a mail carrier and taking his family of six to a game at Fenway wasn't cheap.

I was eight years old sitting on the third base side. I looked out at the Green Monster. Even then I was struck by how it didn't look as tall in person as it did on TV.

I remembered watching the players in the outfield. The way they settled into their spot as if it was the most comfortable place on earth. I remembered watching batters warm up in the batter's box, with their huge, vein-popping forearms. They took those effortless-looking practice swings, but I knew they had the power to send the right pitch a mile over that big green wall in left field.

I remembered the happy chatter my dad engaged

in with nearby fans. I remember his big arm resting over my chair back as we sat together. He'd squeeze my right shoulder every so often. I don't know if I ever felt more loved than I did right then. He must have asked me, "Isn't this something?" at least a dozen times that night. I nodded every time, never saying much, just taking it all in.

I never wanted to leave.

"There's something spiritual about this game," Wally said. "It's more than a job for you and me. It's much more than a paycheck. It's a part of who we are. We get to be part of this thing the way very few people ever get to and there's nowhere else we'd rather be on any given summer night."

He let his words sink in and then asked, "Am I right?"

I nodded and looked up at the clear night sky. My eyes were misty when I opened them.

"Bobby, every day is a gift. This moment is a gift. No matter what happens the rest of the year, live every day to the fullest. Enjoy the moment. Play every game as if it's the last one you'll ever play. Sooner or later, it will be.

"Don't let the business side of this beautiful game

sidetrack you. Don't let any organization take away something so special — something that's a part of who you are.

"Be grateful for every moment you get to be out here. You're a ballplayer and any day you step onto this sacred ground is never wasted. You're part of this game. And nothing can take that away from you."

I heard crickets and the steady hum of the stadium lights. I felt a warm breeze. I was just *here*. Present. Taking it in.

"This is our sacred space," Wally said. "Every individual has a sacred space. That place they know they were born to be a part of. This is that place for you and me. Embrace it. Enjoy it. Be grateful for it.

"**Gratitude is the optimist's greatest weapon. When you're grateful for who you are, where you are, and the very moment you're experiencing, you're able to let go and just be. It doesn't matter what else is going on. You're able to fully experience the present moment. You're able to *play* the game.**

"Give this place your very best every time you're here and I promise you'll never regret a moment of it.

"**There comes a time when a man has to let go of the results and just play. He has to let go of the** outcome he's working for. He can't control it. There are too many variables.

"What he can control is his effort, his attitude, his focus, and his gratitude for the very moment he's experiencing.

"Bobby, **give your very best, keep your mind positive, and be grateful for every opportunity you're blessed with. Do those three things and you *will* be successful**. I don't care what the scoreboard says or what anybody else thinks or does. If a man does those things, he will be successful. That's the only definition of success that matters."

"I hear you loud and clear, Wally. But there's a reason we keep score. If I give my best and fall short of my goals, then my best wasn't good enough."

"Your best is always good enough," Wally said. "Regardless of what the results are, a man can live with the fact that he gave his very best. What a man can't live with is not giving his best and wondering what would have happened if he had. What a man can't live with is growing bitter and developing a pessimistic attitude. What a man can't live with is the regret that he didn't enjoy and embrace every opportunity he was given to do what he loves because he was so caught up in thoughts about the future or the past.

"You can't force the outcomes. You have to give your very best, live in the moment, be grateful for the opportunity, and then accept the outcome."

Wally walked to the pitcher's mound and I followed him.

"Here's something I want you to think about," he said. "It takes about four-tenths of a second for a major league fastball to leave the pitcher's hand and reach home plate. That means a batter must decide whether or not to swing and how he's going to swing in just one-tenth of a second."

We walked to home plate and turned towards the mound.

"Your experience has taught you to process mountains of information in that one-tenth of a second as you try to decipher the pitch and adjust your swing accordingly," Wally said. "But you don't *consciously* process this information. You don't *force* yourself through this step-by-step process.

"It all happens instantly." Wally snapped his fingers. "It all happens at the subconscious level. It happens effortlessly. You don't even think about it because you *can't* consciously think about it.

"In that moment, in that miniscule moment, you don't think about a thing. You don't consciously try to hit a home run. You don't think about what pitch you might see in the future. You don't try to control anything. You just let go, you trust yourself to react, and you live completely in the present moment. You don't control it, you *experience* it. The instant you try to control it, you tighten up and fall apart.

"The same concept must be applied to any other life goal. You have to believe in yourself, you have to trust in yourself, you have to live in each moment…and then you have to let go. That's the hardest part.

"Give your best—always give your very best. Keep your mind in a positive state and be grateful for the opportunity. Experience and enjoy the present moment. As you do, be proud of yourself. *Love* yourself. *Trust* yourself. And then…detach yourself from the results. Let go and trust.

"That's all you can control."

The big stadium lights in the outfield and above the bleachers went out. The lights that remained on cast a soft glow on the infield. I looked around and breathed it all in.

"When you do that," Wally said. "When you do your best, when you're grateful for the moment, when you lose yourself in the moment, and when you let go; you'll feel a sense...of joy...of magic...of peace. A sense of peace that only occurs in a *sacred* space. And when you enter this—this zone—it's been my experience that the outcome will end up better than you ever expected."

31

I spent the rest of August trying to enjoy every moment. My dream of making it back to the majors may have ended and my career may have been coming to an end earlier than I would have liked, but I was determined to do as Wally advised and enjoy every last opportunity I had to play this game I loved.

I remained committed to the positive self-talk techniques Wally had taught me, I continued to focus on the performance goals we had laid out, and I took time each night to visualize myself hitting home runs. But I also made a conscious effort to let go of the things outside of my control and to be grateful for each moment.

I knew that this could be my last season ever as a professional baseball player. These could be the last games I ever played on this sacred ground.

"For the first time since Boston traded me, I'm at peace," I told Janey. "I don't know what will happen next, all I know is I'm going to leave it all on the field. I'm going to go out enjoying every opportunity."

And a funny thing happened. The more I let go, the less I worried about the future, and the more I tried to embrace the moment; the hotter my bat got.

On August 31, I hit my forty-second home run of the season. This broke the modern-era Texas League single-season record—a record that had stood since 1963.

If I was going to go out, I was going to go out swinging.

The last day of August was the most important day of the year for most minor-leaguers. It was the day before major league teams had the option to expand their roster beyond the standard twenty-five players. At least a few guys from every Triple-A team usually got called up to the majors on this day each season.

Some of those guys wouldn't see any playing time, but just one month of a major league salary would be enough to more than double the typical minor-leaguers' salary for the year. Plus, it was an honor. Playing time or not, you had made it to the majors and nobody could ever take that away from you.

These call-ups had a trickle-down effect. Guys in Double-A would get called up to fill those vacant spots in Triple-A, guys in Single-A would get called up to Double-A, and so on. September consisted of only half-a-month or so of games in the minors, but still, a call-up was a call-up and it ended the season on a positive note.

Of course, the September call-ups weren't all winners and no losers. As the rosters were adjusted, some guys would be released to make room for up-and-coming prospects from the lower divisions of minor league baseball.

I wasn't sure if I'd get called up to Omaha for one last stretch or if the organization would simply cut me loose for good. Either way, I was nearly certain that I had played my last game for Northwest Arkansas.

It was another anxious post-game clubhouse as players got called into Wally's office to learn their fate. Two of our teammates got called up to Omaha and we all congratulated them.

My old barroom nemesis, Mitch Mercer, was particularly loud and obnoxious on this night. He was letting everyone know his predictions on who was going up and who was going down. It was tasteless and annoying. It only added to the anxiety in the clubhouse.

"I'll tell you something right now, I gotta feelin'

that Bobby Kane here is going to get his call-up," he said to anyone who would listen. His prediction surprised me. We had been cordial to each other and exchanged in-game fist bumps here and there ever since our melee back in June, but friends we were not.

"You think so?" I said. "I appreciate that."

"But don't kid yourselves," Mitch continued. "He's getting what's called a *good-guy* call-up. The organization tries to give one of the old guys one final month at a higher level before sending him on his way. One last trot along the bases. Ain't that right, Bobby?"

I shook my head and tried to smile it off — show that I could take some ribbing.

Mitch wasn't wrong. There was such a thing as a "good-guy promotion." A club would call somebody up to the majors who had put in several years in Triple-A so that he could get one month of a big-league salary on his way out. It was a thank-you gesture from the organization for the years he put in. However, I wasn't aware of this happening at levels below Triple-A. The difference in one month's pay between Triple-A and Double-A wasn't all that significant. If anything, asking a Double-A player to pack his bags and go spend his final few games in a new Triple-A town for not much more money wasn't much of a gift.

"Mercer," one of the assistant coaches yelled. "Wally wants to see you."

Mitch smiled big as he trotted down the hall. "Later, boys. It's been fun."

This one stung. I could be happy for just about every other teammate of mine getting called up, but Mitch? This guy was supposed to be the other power hitter on the team—my closest competition—and I had *tripled* his fourteen home runs. My batting average of .309 was third-best in the Texas League and his was way down the list at .231.

Plus, Mitch was, quite frankly, the biggest jerk in the clubhouse.

This was a slap in the face.

I tried to tell myself that Mitch was getting called up because the organization had invested so much in him. Because he was younger. Because the team had more to lose if he didn't develop into the player they had paid so much money for.

These rationalizations were tough to swallow. It wasn't right. I was a better ballplayer than him, regardless of age. I deserved a call-up before he did.

After a couple minutes, I heard Wally's office door swing open and I swallowed my pride. I told myself I needed to do the right thing. I needed to be the bigger man.

I saw Mitch return with a reddened face, the kind you get when you're trying to suppress tears.

I stood up and extended my hand.

"Mitch," I said. "Congratulations. No hard feelings and best of luck to you."

"Get out of my face," he said.

His response startled me and I noticed his right fist heading quickly towards my face. I ducked back just in time for him to barely miss me. I regained my composure and tackled the bigger man rugby style. The clubhouse erupted into chaos as the two of us once again found ourselves wrestling on the ground. Our teammates pulled us apart before either of us got injured.

"Knock it off!" I heard Wally yell as teammates held us back from each other.

"Get off me," Mitch screamed in a high-pitched shrill at the players holding his arms.

"Mitch," Wally yelled. "Show some class."

"Mind your own business, Wally," Mitch snapped. "You can't tell me what to do anymore. Nobody can." He was throwing a childlike tantrum.

It was then that I realized what had happened. Mitch's reddened face wasn't the sign of joyful tears to come, it was rage.

He hadn't been called up. He had been released from the team.

"Bobby," Wally said. "Step into my office."

32

A combination of adrenaline still pumping from my skirmish with Mitch and nerves twisting in my stomach made for an ugly combination. My legs felt wobbly as I followed Wally back to his office. When I closed the door and took a seat, I held on tight and tried to steady myself.

I was sweating, my face felt hot, and my hands were shaky. I'd been in this situation before, sitting in the manager's office waiting to hear my fate. But this was the most intense my nerves had ever been.

"What was that about?" Wally asked.

"I thought he had been called up," I said, though my voice didn't sound like mine. It was almost like I was observing this conversation from a distance.

"Whoops," Wally said with a slight smile. "That guy's got problems. His contract was up for renewal and I guess his agent still thinks he's worth millions. The organization has lost patience with him. I never liked him, but he'll land somewhere. Hopefully this is a wakeup call for him."

I nodded. At that moment, Mitch's wellbeing and the future of *his* career wasn't exactly at the forefront of my mind.

"You know why you're in here," Wally said.

I nodded again.

I had rehearsed what I was going to say to Wally at this moment. Regardless of what he was about to tell me, I wanted to let him know how much I appreciated all he had done for me. How I was going to miss him. How I knew this wasn't his decision and he had done everything he possibly could to help me. How I'd be forever grateful for him changing my life the way he had. But I couldn't speak.

"What you did this season was one of the most amazing things I've ever seen," Wally said. His face was set in stone. All business. "Where you were in May compared to where you are now—it's just unbelievable. No matter where you go or what you do in the future, you gave everything you had this season and I'll never forget that. You're a special guy, Bobby. Whatever you decide to do in life will be something great. That, I know. Don't stop believing in yourself."

"Thanks," I finally said. My voice dry and quiet. I could see where this was going.

"Here," Wally said as he slid something across his desk towards me. I looked down and saw that it was a plane ticket. "This is for you."

The destination: Boston.

"The organization wants to send you home," he said.

This was it. The end of my career.

And this is how it ends? I thought to myself.

I knew this day would come. I had prepared myself for it as best as I could. But I suppose you can never truly be ready for a moment like this.

I felt like I'd been holding my breath for the past minute and I finally exhaled. Good or bad, there was some relief to the finality of it all.

"Let me guess," I said. "As a token of appreciation, the organization is paying for my plane ticket back to Boston. For all the years of hard work, they'll cover the two-hundred-dollar plane ride that leaves…" I looked at the ticket. "Tonight? Of course. How thoughtful. Surely I can pack up everything I have in an hour or two and be on my way, right?"

I shook my head and pushed the ticket back to Wally.

"They can keep it," I said. "I'll drive home."

"You don't understand," Wally said. "You need to be in Boston tonight."

At that moment, I saw a hint of a smile work its way up one side of Wally's face.

"Why?" I asked, with the sudden realization that I was missing something.

"Because that's where the Royals are playing tomorrow and they want you in the lineup."

I couldn't speak. I wanted Wally to repeat what he just said. I wanted to be sure I heard it correctly. But I couldn't say anything.

"You're going to the bigs, Bobby."

I inhaled deep, exhaled heavy, put my head in my hands, and covered my eyes as the tears flowed.

Wally came around from his desk and I felt him slap my back.

"Oh, and by the way, if you didn't already know this, you're now in the middle of a pennant race."

33

"I'm heading to Boston right now," I told Janey on the phone as I drove to the airport. "Think you can meet me there tomorrow?"

Silence. Then I heard her say, very softly, "Oh, Bobby. I'm so sorry. You worked so hard. I'm so sorry."

I smiled and said, "And could you wear blue when you get there?"

"You want me to wear blue when I meet you—"

She stopped herself.

"Bobby, what are you saying?"

"I need you wearing blue because I'm suiting up for the Royals to play against the Red Sox tomorrow."

I heard her scream, I heard her cry, and I heard her tell our kids and her parents the news. Then I heard them screaming—and maybe a few cries from our boys, who had no idea what was going on.

Just listening to this joyous chaos was one of the greatest moments of my life.

"You did it," Janey said to me above the

commotion. "I'm so proud of you. You did it! You did it!"

"We did it," I said, holding back tears of my own. "*We* did it!"

34

The next twenty-four hours was a dream. A wonderful, chaotic dream.

The Royals were leading the American League Central Division and fighting to ensure a postseason spot. Every game from here on out was crucial.

When I met up with the Royals in Boston, the first thing Royals Manager Ned Yost said to me was, "This isn't a good-guy promotion, just so you know. This is the real deal. We're trying to make the postseason and we need you to come through for us. We're counting on you."

"Yes, sir," I said. "I'm ready."

Ned had an easygoing personality and the Royals were a tight group that welcomed me right away. I received nothing but support from everyone in the clubhouse.

That night in Fenway Park, I was told to be ready to pinch hit if the opportunity arose.

In the ninth inning, I got that opportunity.

We were trailing, 6-4, and had two on base. There

were two outs. Talk about being thrown into the fire. If I didn't get a hit, the game was over. This was a moment that would undoubtedly let the team know whether or not I could handle the pressure of major league baseball.

Prior to my at-bat, as I warmed up in the on-deck circle, I gave Janey and my family a nod. When they heard the news, they had all rushed to find tickets. Janey, my two boys, her parents, my mom, my two sisters, and my little brother were all sitting on the third-base side — not far from where we had sat as a family when were kids. I could almost see my dad sitting with them all.

I walked to the batter's box and the first thing I noticed was the noise. It was louder, *much* louder, but in a good way. It was less distracting. In the minors, it wasn't uncommon to hear a few people on the other side of the stadium having a loud conversation that had nothing to do with baseball. Here, there was a loud buzz. There was energy in the air.

The fans were on their feet chanting, "Let's go Red Sox!" They were one out away from a victory and they were hoping I would be that out.

I fed off the energy. Even though it wasn't intended

to pump *me* up, the loud crowd lifted me. I felt ten-feet tall with a bat that could summon the power of Zeus.

I pictured myself swinging at the first pitch and I saw it going over the Green Monster in left field, just as I'd envisioned it as a kid. I felt so alive—so full of power—that I just knew I'd be sending the ball either over or *through* the Green Monster.

The pitcher must have known I was charged up. He threw me a high, high fastball on the first pitch and I swung away.

Missing wildly.

I swung so hard I actually twisted myself up and tripped forward, nearly falling over as the crowd roared their approval.

Okay, not what I expected. I need to relax.

The next pitch was a changeup and I swung again…this time *way* out in front.

I stepped out of the batter's box, took a deep breath, and told myself, *I can hit off this guy. His fastball was made for me. I've earned my spot to be here. Don't overthink it, Bobby. Just play. Let go and trust. PLAY the game you love.*

His next pitch was a wicked slider, but I managed

to foul it off. He followed that up with another, which I also fouled off.

Then came a high fastball. This time I laid off it and got my first ball.

The next pitch went way outside for ball two.

I fouled off another changeup and the next pitch was a slider in the dirt for ball three.

Full count.

I had worked the count like a seasoned pro, if I may say so myself.

I've got him rattled, I thought. *I can see it. He doesn't want to load the bases by walking this guy fresh out of Double-A. He's rattled and he wants to put me away here. When a pitcher with heat gets rattled, he always goes back to the heat. The fastball is coming. I can feel it. Let go and trust yourself. Just PLAY.*

I was right. He threw me a mean fastball, a bit inside, and I swung away.

That sound. Even above the crowd noise, there was no mistaking *that sound.*

My ball lifted and lifted toward left field. The Green Monster, which always looked shorter in person than it did on TV, suddenly looked about twenty-feet higher than I ever remembered it. They say it's thirty-seven feet and two inches tall, but it looked at least fifty feet high at this moment.

I put my head down and ran like hell.

I was rounding first when I looked up and couldn't find the ball. I saw the Red Sox players sagging with no sense of urgency and I saw my third base coach smiling big as he casually waved me to keep going.

It had cleared the Green Monster.

My first major league at-bat in eight years and I hit a home run with the game on the line. And I did it on the very field where I'd had three errors the last time I was here.

We won the game that night, 7-6.

35

I called Wally after my Kansas City debut and he picked up right away. He was excited and proud. I told him all the things I had wanted to tell him before — how much I appreciated all he had done for me.

"Don't go talking like the story is over," Wally said. "Remember our original plan. Once you get to the majors in September, you have to prove you *belong* there. I know you can do it, but don't lose your focus. Don't stop believing."

As September wore on and we continued to fight for a playoff spot, I was put in at various times as the pinch hitter. Baseball is difficult enough when you only get four or five at-bats a night, but it's considerably harder when you only get *one* at-bat in a given night.

I did the best I could to stay relaxed and poised in these high-pressure situations. The home run at Fenway was the highlight of my month, but I still managed to get on base four more times in ten at-bats.

With four games to go, Ned Yost told me he was inserting me in the lineup as the right fielder. I had earned the team's trust and a spot in the starting lineup.

Over those final four games, I hit two more home runs. My September total fell well short of the goal Wally and I had originally set, but my season wasn't over. We earned a playoff spot and began our best-of-five American League Division Series against the Houston Astros.

The series went to a winner-take-all Game Five; whichever team won would advance to the American League Championship Series.

I started in right field for the entire series against Houston. I didn't do anything particularly memorable until Game Five.

In my first at-bat of the day, I hit one to the wall at Kaufman Stadium and earned my first triple in the majors.

In the third inning, I hit one just over the shortstop's head and made it to first for a single.

The third time I stepped to the plate, I crushed the ball deep into left field for a double.

I had gone three-for-three in the biggest game of

my short major league career. And I was a home run away from "hitting for the cycle." This is an extremely-rare and highly-coveted baseball feat where a batter hits a single, a double, a triple, and a home run in one game. Hitting for the cycle is about as uncommon for a batter as a pitcher throwing a no-hitter. It's a cherished record. As of the 2015 postseason, it had only happened 304 times in 133 years of major league baseball.

It had *never* been done in a postseason game.

I came to the plate in the eighth inning with a chance to make history. We were down, 5-4, with two on base. This was going to be my moment. I was going to complete the cycle and I was going to give our team the lead in the process.

Or, so I thought.

As I stepped into the batter's box, the Astros' pitcher looked at me and smiled. He then intentionally walked me. My once-in-a-lifetime opportunity had been taken away. I couldn't believe it. Everyone in the stadium knew what I was on the verge of doing.

It was the smart baseball move, but our hometown fans let Houston have it.

The pitcher struck out the next batter and ended

the inning—along with my chances of making baseball history.

But then, the baseball gods smiled on me. We tied things up in the ninth inning and the game went into extra innings.

The entire season was riding on every pitch as we battled it out in the tenth, then the eleventh.

In the twelfth inning, I stepped to the plate. The game was tied, 5-5. I wasn't thinking about the cycle at this point. All I wanted to do was get on base, to keep our season alive.

I made eye contact with the pitcher and I saw that the pressure was on him. He didn't want to be the guy pitching when baseball history was made. He didn't want to be the guy who gave up the game-winner to a Double-A player. He was in trouble. I knew it and he knew it.

I swung at the first pitch. I felt nothing, but I heard *that sound*. The ball sailed over the right-center wall and landed in the famous fountains at Kaufman Stadium. I've been told it traveled 470 feet.

The stadium erupted. My teammates dogpiled on me after I crossed home plate. Our catcher poured Gatorade on me during the postgame interview.

It was a walk-off homer. It was the first time ever that a player hit for the cycle in a postseason game. And it was the game-winner that advanced us to the American League Championship Series.

It was the kind of thing that seems so farfetched you don't even dare to dream it. But like Wally told me, **when you aim high, stay positive, enjoy the moment, let go of the results, and trust yourself; the outcome will end up better than you ever expected**.

36

On November 1, 2015, we beat the New York Mets in Game Five of the World Series to win Kansas City's first world championship since 1985. It wasn't lost on me that Wally was a member of that 1985 team.

As I look back, the whole thing is just bizarre. It's hard to believe it happened. In two months, I went from Double-A baseball and thinking I was about to be forced into retirement to hitting a home run over the Green Monster, hitting for the cycle in the postseason (something no other player in major league baseball history had ever done), and winning a World Series ring with the Kansas City Royals.

I ended up hitting seven home runs during my late-season stint in the majors. With the forty-two I hit during my time in the Texas League, I fell one short of the fifty total we had set as a goal for the season. But like Wally said, "**If you aim high and fall short, you're still going to land higher than you've ever landed before.**"

Who could argue with that?

During this two-month whirlwind of a dream come true, another statement Wally made kept running through my head.

"It's a funny thing," Wally had told me one night in the dugout during one of our Texas League games. **"The luckier I think I am, the luckier I become**."

I guess the Royals believed what I had done during my two months in the majors was more than luck because as soon as the season ended, they offered me a three-year deal for nearly $3 million.

They say the only constant in life is change. I'm proof of that. No matter where you are right now, you may do a complete 180 two months from now. That's certainly what happened to me.

The only thing we can control is how we respond to all that change. That's what Wally Hogan taught me.

We get to choose whether we respond with an optimistic outlook and a positive, can-do attitude, or with a pessimistic outlook and a negative, what's-the-use attitude.

How we choose to respond to life's changing moments determines our outcome.

I don't know what's next in my life. I don't know

how long I'll be playing in the majors or what I'll do after that chapter of my life is closed. But I do know how I'll respond to whatever comes next—with optimism.

Anyone can be optimistic when things are going well. Anyone can be positive for a moment, a day, or a week. But it's a *commitment* to positive thinking that makes the difference—a promise to yourself to permanently change the way you respond to the endless series of negative events we all experience. *That's* what makes the difference.

When you commit yourself to positive thinking, *everything* changes.

Bibliography & Recommended Resources

Learned Optimism: How to Change Your Mind and Your Life by Martin E. P. Seligman

How Champions Think: In Sports and in Life by Dr. Bob Rotella with Bob Cullen

The Magic of Thinking Big by David J. Schwartz

The Happiness Advantage: The Seven Principles of Positive Psychology That Fuel Success and Performance at Work by Shawn Achor

Psycho-Cybernetics by Maxwell Maltz

Mind Gym: An Athlete's Guide to Inner Excellence by Gary Mack with David Casstevens

Where Nobody Knows Your Name: Life in the Minor Leagues of Baseball by John Feinstein

Tommy Lasorda: My Way by Colin Gunderson

Life Is Yours to Win: Lessons Forged from the Purpose, Passion, and Magic of Baseball by Augie Garrido

When You Come to a Fork in the Road, Take It!: Inspiration and Wisdom From One of Baseball's Greatest Heroes by Yogi Berra with Dave Kaplan

The Life You Imagine: Life Lessons for Achieving Your Dreams by Derek Jeter

I Was Right On Time by Buck O'Neil with Steve Wulf and David Conrads

About the Author

DARRIN DONNELLY is the bestselling author of *Think Like a Warrior*, *Relentless Optimism*, and several others books in the inspirational *Sports for the Soul* series. Though the main characters in Donnelly's books are usually coaches or athletes, they represent anyone with a big dream and the desire to be successful. The seasons and games they endure represent the seasons of life we all must go through when trying to master a new skill, achieve a new goal, or rebound from a setback.

Sports for the Soul books help readers fill their minds with motivation and positivity while also learning how to build confidence, overcome adversity, and achieve their goals—in all areas of life.

Donnelly lives in Kansas City with his wife and three children.

He can be reached at SportsForTheSoul.com and on Twitter @DarrinDonnelly.

Sports for the Soul

This book is part of the *Sports for the Soul* series. For updates on this book, a sneak peek at future books, and a free newsletter that delivers powerful advice and inspiration from top coaches, athletes, and sports psychologists, join us at: **SportsForTheSoul.com**.

The *Sports for the Soul* newsletter will help you:

- Find your purpose and follow your passion

- Use a positive mental attitude to achieve more

- Build your self-confidence

- Develop mental toughness

- Increase your energy and stay motivated

- Harness the power of positive self-talk

- Explore the spiritual side of success

- Be a positive leader for your family and your team

- Become the best version of yourself

- And much more…

Join us now at **SportsForTheSoul.com**.

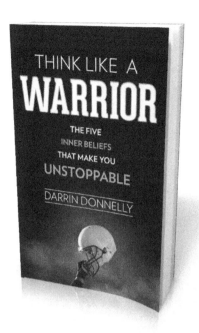

Think Like a Warrior

by Darrin Donnelly

In this bestselling inspirational fable, a college football coach at the end of his rope receives mysterious visits from five of history's greatest coaches: **John Wooden, Buck O'Neil, Herb Brooks, Bear Bryant, and Vince Lombardi**. Together, these legendary leaders teach him the five inner beliefs shared by the world's most successful people. The "warrior mindset" he develops changes his life forever — and it will change yours as well.

Old School Grit

by Darrin Donnelly

An old-school college basketball coach who thinks like John Wooden and talks like Mike Ditka enters the final NCAA tournament of his legendary career and uses his last days as a coach to write letters to the next generation revealing his rules for a happy and successful life: the 15 rules of grit. Consider this book an instruction manual for getting back to the values that truly lead to success and developing the type of old school grit that will get you through anything.

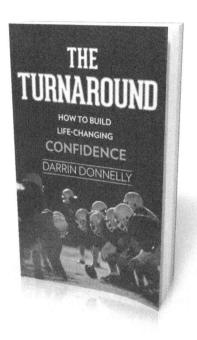

The Turnaround

by Darrin Donnelly

Danny O'Connor is an insecure fourth-string quarterback on one of the worst college football teams in America. But his life changes when a new coach is hired and begins showing Danny and his teammates how to build the confidence needed to turn around their losing ways. As this story plays out, you will learn the practical, real-world methods used by some of the greatest coaches of all time for instantly generating self-confidence.

Collect all six books in the
Sports for the Soul series...

For more information, visit SportsForTheSoul.com

Made in the USA
Las Vegas, NV
29 June 2021